The Cornell Book of Herbs and Edible Flowers

THE CORNELL BOOK of HERBS & edible flowers

Cornell Cooperative Extension
Ithaca, New York

Produced by Media Services at Cornell University

Project Director	James A. Mason
Editor	Trudie Calvert
Designer	Wendy Kenigsberg
Photographer	Bruce Wang, Cornell University Photography
Production Coordinator	Donna Vantine

Typeface	Adobe Goudy Old Style
Printer	Finger Lakes Press, Auburn, New York
Paper	Warren Lustro Gloss Recycled 80 lb. text and 100 lb. cover
Endpapers	Cross Pointe, Genesis, Tallow 80 lb. text

Copyright © 1993 Cornell University
Cornell Cooperative Extension provides equal program and employment opportunities.
✺ Printed on recycled paper

132HB 1181/1695 4/93 FLP 15M E10216G

In some of the descriptions of herbs, medicinal uses are mentioned. This information is not meant as a substitute for a doctor's care and advice or for prescribed medicines. Do not use this book to self-diagnose or self-treat a health problem.

For Heather Mackin, with love

Contents

ix	Acknowledgments	52	Parsley—*Petroselinum crispum*
xi	Introduction	54	Roman Chamomile—*Chamaemelum nobile* (*Anthemis nobilis*)
2	Angelica—*Angelica archangelica*		
4	Anise Hyssop—*Agastache foeniculum*	56	Rosemary—*Rosmarinus officinalis*
6	Borage—*Borago officinalis*	58	Rue—*Ruta graveolens*
8	Caraway—*Carum carvi*	60	Salad Burnet—*Poterium sanguisorba* (*Sanguisorba minor*)
10	Chervil—*Anthriscus cerefolium*	62	Scented Geranium—*Pelargonium*
12	Chives—*Allium schoenoprasum*		Lemon Geranium—*Pelargonium crispum*
14	Clary Sage—*Salvia sclarea*		Rose Geranium—*Pelargonium graveolens*
16	Common Fennel—*Foeniculum vulgare*	64	Apple Geranium—*Pelargonium odoratissimum*
18	Common Wormwood—*Artemisia absinthium*		Peppermint Geranium—*Pelargonium tomentosum*
20	Coriander—*Coriandrum sativum*	66	Southernwood—*Artemisia abrotanum*
22	Dill—*Anethum graveolens*	68	Summer Savory—*Satureja hortensis*
24	Dittany of Crete—*Origanum dictamnus* (*Amaracus dictamnus*)	70	Sweet Basil—*Ocimum basilicum*
		72	Sweet Cicely/Myrrh—*Myrrhis odorata*
26	French Tarragon—*Artemisia dracunculus* 'French'	74	Sweet Marjoram—*Origanum majorana* (*Majorana hortensis*)
28	Garden Sage—*Salvia officinalis*		
30	Germander—*Teucrium chamaedrys*	76	Sweet Woodruff—*Galium odoratum*
32	Horehound—*Marrubium vulgare*	78	Tansy—*Tanacetum vulgare*
34	Horseradish—*Armoracia rusticana*	80	Thyme—*Thymus*
36	Hyssop—*Hyssopus officinalis*	84	True Lavender—*Lavandula angustifolia* (*L. vera*; *L. officinalis*)
38	Lady's Mantle—*Alchemilla vulgaris*		
40	Lavender Cotton—*Santolina chamaecyparissus* (*S. incana*)	86	Wild Marjoram/Oregano—*Origanum vulgare*
		88	Winter Savory—*Satureja montana*
42	Lemon Balm—*Melissa officinalis*	90	Yarrow/Milfoil—*Achillea millefolium*
44	Lemon Verbena—*Aloysia triphylla* (*Lippia citriodora*)	94	Bee Balm—*Monarda didyma*
		96	Calendula/Pot Marigold—*Calendula officinalis*
46	Lovage—*Levisticum officinale*	98	Daylily—*Hemerocallis*
48	Mint—*Mentha* Peppermint—*Mentha* x *piperita*	100	Nasturtium—*Tropaeolum majus*
		102	Rose—*Rosa*
50	Corsican Mint—*Mentha requienii* Spearmint—*Mentha spicata*	104	Viola: Sweet Violet—*Viola odorata* Johnny Jump-Up—*Viola tricolor* Pansy—*Viola* x *Wittrockiana*

An herbal wreath, made by Alison Wiley of Littleflowers in Newfield, New York, uses sage, thyme, lemon thyme, winter savory, parsley, French tarragon, apple mint, pineapple mint, bee balm, and chive flowers.

Other dried herbs that can be used in wreaths are tansy, geranium, lady's mantle, wild marjoram, rosemary, lavender, lavender cotton, rue, and yarrow.

Acknowledgments

Many generous people provided support and materials for this book: Harriet B. Flannery and Robert G. Mower, authors of an earlier Cornell Cooperative Extension publication on herbs; Diane Miske of Cornell Plantations for professional consultation and photographs of coriander, mints, and sweet woodruff; Christina Stark, Division of Nutritional Sciences, Cornell University; David O. Watkins provided the photograph of daylilies; Elaine Engst, Margaret Rogers, and Laura Linke of the Division of Rare and Manuscript Collections, Kroch Library, Cornell University Library; and Edward A. Cope of the L. H. Bailey Hortorium, Cornell University. Members of the Media Services editorial and design staff offered artistic and emotional support.

Within the community, Dorry Baird Norris of Sage Cottage in Trumansburg opened her house and garden to us; Alison Wiley of Littleflowers allowed generous use of her drying barn; David Drogo assisted in food preparation. Others provided props, materials, and gardens: Margaret Fabrizzio and the Ithaca High School Herb Garden; Pam Connett of Butternut Canning; Julie Tubbs of Heartstrings; the Archway Bed and Breakfast; Richard T. Hess Pottery; Roxanne Dragovich of Winsome Winds; S. K. List; Contemporary Trends; Oasis Ware; the Plantation; and Gloria Barrett of Turn of the Century Antiques.

Last but very far from least, my special thanks to designer Wendy Kenigsberg for her imaginative and lovely work, and to copy editor Trudie Calvert.

A garden is as new today as when men and women first grew plants, long before history was recorded. It comes fresh from seeds and roots, grown of new rains and sunshine, sprung from the tireless earth. The experience is different in every season. New hopes are to be fulfilled. New kinds of plants are to be grown. We are relieved from the turmoil in which mankind lives, comforted by the calmness of silent, growing things. A garden maintains our faith and confidence. ✳︎ —Liberty Hyde Bailey

Introduction

Herbs, according to popular wisdom, can flavor a roast, repel mice, or keep your love true, depending on which problem is most urgent and which herb is used. No wonder herb gardens are enjoying a newfound popularity.

Like all useful and wonderful things, this Eden-old agricultural concept periodically blazes anew, lighting fires of inspiration. Herb gardens have been beautifying dwellings and improving the diet since the earliest times, when we first learned that herbs could make the day's catch more palatable.

Many millennia later, we still feel we have dined better if the food has been flavored with herbs. And we're right to feel so. Herbs were the world's first vitamins and medicines. Long before antistress vitamins were discovered, chamomile was brewed into a golden tea to calm the nerves. Long before today's medicines were developed, the ancients used horehound to soothe a cough or a lovage tea to ease rheumatism. Long before monosodium glutamate was introduced to jolt the taste buds, good cooks used herbs such as sage and dill to make meals tasty and digestible.

Strewing basil seed the traditional way, with shouts and curses, lets off steam outdoors and may be one reason for its reputation for safeguarding the home. It would be hard to prove that a spouse was kept faithful through the influence of an herb. Country dwellers, however, can speak for mint's ability to keep mice out of the cupboards.

What better place to obtain herbs than from the home garden, where they can be picked fresh as needed?

Herb gardens, like the herbs themselves, have been a constant in numerous cultures, sometimes vigorous and thriving, other times of diminished interest, but always there in some form or another.

The ancient Greeks preferred to plant their herbs in natural garden settings, complete with springs and trees, or to gather wild herbs from the countryside. Medieval monks planted tidy, raised beds of herbs that were more useful than lovely, as if to keep at bay the chaos outside their cloister. In the Renaissance, herbs that provided flowers and sweet fragrance were esteemed by dainty, genteel folk. In the seventeenth and eighteenth centuries, European gardeners planted curious finds from the New World such as the potato. (Botanically, an herb is any plant that dies back to the ground each year, including many we think of as vegetables or flowers.) The colonists brought precious boxes of Old World herbs for their New World gardens, and some of them, such as goldenrod, quickly escaped to field and roadside, changing our landscape forever. Victorians liked their herb beds formal and sentimental, filling them with sweet violets and lavender.

Today, an herb garden can be anything from a few herbs grown in pots on a windowsill to a formal knot garden complete with box hedges. Herb gardens, like enduring friendships, adapt and adjust to circumstances.

More than fifty herbs are described in this book. Dioscorides, in the first century A.D., included five hundred plants in his herbal. This one is limited to familiar and usually easily grown herbs. Most are potherbs used for culinary purposes, but some have domestic uses outside the kitchen, and others are simply beautiful to see and sniff.

Beginning gardeners may want to plant a few of their favorites in a small plot that can be enlarged over the years. Herbs can be introduced into existing gardens, adding a variety of foliage colors and blooms to plantings of annuals, perennials, and shrubs.

Some herb gardens are arranged by theme: a kitchen herb garden, a fragrance garden, a medicinal garden, or even a gray garden, consisting solely of herbs with silvery-gray foliage.

If space or permanence of the current dwelling is a problem, many herbs can be grown in pots.

More ambitious gardeners may want to try the Victorian herb garden devised by the American horticulturist Liberty Hyde Bailey, who included in his writings a plan for an abundant herb border that provides potherbs and flowers for much of the year.

Two carpet-bed designs from Liberty Hyde Bailey's 1906 edition of Garden-Making. *He writes, "The beauty of the carpet-bed lies largely in its unity, sharp contrast and harmony of color, elegance—often simplicity—of design, nicety of execution, and the continued distinctness of outline due to scrupulous care."*

Liberty Hyde Bailey (1858–1954) was a professor and then dean at the New York State College of Agriculture at Cornell University from 1888 until his retirement in 1913. He was a botanist, educator, scientist, world traveler, and author of scores of books. He changed the way people view gardens and gardening by repeatedly stressing humanity's oneness with the world and the need to live at peace with ourselves and our surroundings—even with weeds. "A garden," he wrote, "requires labor and attention. Plants do not grow merely to satisfy ambitions or to fulfill good intentions. They thrive because some one expended effort on them."

A garden, for Bailey, could be as large as a field or as small as a pot, and even the humblest of plants was worthy of admiration and care; the important thing was that the garden be a place of reflection, education, and spiritual nourishment. Liberty Hyde Bailey's thoughts on gardening and gardeners are scattered throughout this book. Direct quotes from Bailey are set off in small type and identified by the initials LHB. I hope other readers enjoy them as much as I did.

Bailey on his travels.

1882
Bailey at twenty-four with his red collecting case.

The collage to the right includes Liberty Hyde Bailey memorabilia housed at Cornell University (clockwise): red collecting case (vasculum); Stetson hat; Hortus and three of Bailey's many books; scrapbook from a trip to Venezuela and Trinidad in 1920–21; a specimen of sage (Salvia officinalis) collected in 1924; an envelope of chervil seeds; three of the many canes Bailey collected in his travels; and a page from Hortus Third.

Liberty Hyde Bailey described the Victorian herb garden he recommended for the home:

> Every family garden should have a border permanently set aside for sweet herbs. A strip of land four feet wide and fifty feet long will ordinarily be ample, allowing the growing of clumps of all the leading kinds of sweet, aromatic and condimental plants. One end or section of the border should be reserved for the perennial species, and the remainder for the annuals (Those that must be re-sown each year.)
>
> The perennial sweet herbs may be propagated by division, although they are usually grown from seeds. The second year—and sometimes even the first year—the plants are strong enough for cutting. Even with the perennial kinds, it is advisable to renew or re-sow the plants every few years, to prevent the beds from running out. The common perennial sweet herbs are: Sage, lavender, peppermint, spearmint, hyssop, thyme, marjoram, balm, catnip, rosemary, horehound, fennel, lovage, winter savory, tansy, wormwood, costmary.
>
> The commoner annual species (or those which are treated as annuals) are: Anise, sweet basil, summer savory, coriander, pennyroyal, caraway (biennial), clary (biennial), dill (biennial), sweet marjoram (biennial).

Herbs, like many wonderful things, can be difficult to define. For the purposes of this book, an herb is any plant or plant part that has historically been used, or is used today, for culinary, medicinal, fragrant, or other household purposes.

General Culture

Most herbs thrive in sunny locations, in good garden loam with neutral pH and good drainage. There are exceptions, of course, such as angelica and woodruff, which prefer partial shade. Once established, most herbs do best in dry soil and need watering only during drought. A few, however, such as mint and lovage, prefer moist soil. Be sure to plant herbs in locations best suited to their needs. This is easy to do: there are herbs that thrive in every situation—wet or dry, sun or shade.

Most herbs do not require fertilization except for heavily harvested ones such as basil, chives, and parsley.

Before planting the herb bed, work the soil to a depth of one foot or more, breaking up large clods and adding organic matter if the soil is heavy or shallow. Keep the plantings free of weeds over the growing season. Consider using a mulch of wood chips, shredded bark, buckwheat hulls, or cocoa beans to discourage weeds and provide winter protection.

Propagation

Herbs are variously propagated from seed, stem cuttings, division, or layering. They can be obtained from nurseries or in the traditional manner from friends who are thinning their herb gardens.

Sewing Seed Outdoors

In the spring, after all danger of frost is past and the soil is warm and has begun to dry, sow seeds at a depth of twice their diameter. Broadcast very small seeds on the surface and lightly cover with finely sifted soil. Firm the soil and moisten with a fine spray of water. Keep the soil moist but not soggy until seeds germinate.

When two true leaves develop, thin the seedlings that have been sown in place to the proper spacing by removing the smaller, weaker ones. This may seem harsh, but it is necessary. Or transplant flat-grown seedlings into the garden. Transplanting is best done on a cloudy day or in late afternoon. Leave a good clump of soil around the seedlings when moving them and water them right after transplanting.

If seeds are sown in autumn, it should be late in the season so they will not germinate before frost. Follow the same techniques as for spring sowing.

Sowing Seed Indoors

For many herbs, gardeners can get a head start on the growing season by planting seeds indoors. Don't start too early, though, or you'll end up with spindly, weak plants. Eight weeks before the last average date of the last frost is time enough.

Any clean, deep container with drainage holes can be used. Flats, the most common container for starting seeds, are available from garden supply stores. The seeding medium can be commercially purchased or homemade by combining shredded sphagnum peat moss and fine-grade (#4) vermiculite in equal proportions. Fill the container, firm the seeding medium, and moisten it with a fine spray of water.

Make shallow rows two or three inches apart; sow the seeds evenly at the same depth as for outdoor sowing or according to the directions on the package. Label the rows with the names of the herbs and the date of sowing. Place the container in a pan with two inches of water and remove it when moisture becomes visible on the surface. Or water from the top with a

very fine spray. Place the container in a plastic bag in a warm, well-lighted location or under fluorescent lights. Don't put it in direct sunlight.

As soon as the seeds have germinated, remove the plastic bag and put the container in full sun or under fluorescent lights six to eight inches from the seedlings. Rotate the container every day or two if the seedlings start to bend toward the light. Herbs that grow slowly and are not ready to be transplanted when quicker-growing ones are ready should be fertilized every ten days with a dilute solution of a water-soluble fertilizer.

Seedlings, unfortunately, are prone to damping-off, a soilborne fungus. The disease thrives under excessive soil moisture, poor air circulation, and warm temperature. Good growing conditions, plus a commercial fungicide, will protect the plants.

When two true leaves appear, the seedlings can be transplanted to small pots or wider spacing in flats. Use a commercial potting soil. When transplanting, disturb the roots as little as possible. Make a hole in the leveled, moistened soil with your finger; pick up a single seedling, leaving a small ball of soil around the roots; and lower the seedling into the hole. Firm the soil and water gently. Keep the container in light shade for a day or two after transplanting and be sure the soil is moist while the transplants recover.

When herbs are ready to be transplanted outdoors (usually after the last frost, when the soil has begun to warm), place them in a cold frame or partially shaded, protected outdoor area for a few days. Gradually expose them to full sun, and after a few days transplant them into the garden.

Stem Cuttings

Some herbs, such as lavender, rosemary, scented geraniums, and lemon balm, can be propagated by stem cuttings. Take cuttings of strong, new tip growth during the spring or summer from healthy, established plants. Make the cut with a sharp knife or pruning shears just below a node, where a leaf joins the stem. The cuttings should be three to five inches long and contain two or more nodes. Wrap the cuttings in a damp cloth so they stay cool and moist until they are planted.

A mixture of sphagnum peat moss and #2 vermiculite in equal proportions makes a good rooting medium for stem cuttings. Any container can be used as long as it is clean and provides drainage. Fill the container with moist rooting medium and firm it down. Remove all leaves from the bottom two inches of the cutting and any flowers or buds from the top. Rooting hormone can be applied to the cut end of the stem but is not necessary. Put the stems into the medium, firm the soil around the cuttings, and water thoroughly. Cover with a plastic bag and put under strong natural light or fluorescent lights but not in direct sun. The cuttings will develop roots in two to four weeks; during this time, open the bag periodically to provide air circulation and make sure the soil stays moist. The cuttings can be transplanted when they have developed a dense, fibrous root system. Before transplanting them into the garden, gradually acclimate them to the outdoor environment, as described above for seedlings.

Layering

Herbs such as santolina, thyme, sage, and winter savory can be propagated by layering, a technique to produce roots on a stem that is attached to the parent plant. Select a vigorous branch growing close to the ground or one flexible enough to bend down to the soil. Holding the branch close to the soil, bend the last six inches of the stem back into a vertical position. Gently scrape the underside of the bent branch where it is closest to the soil. Bury that scraped, bent portion three to six inches deep and anchor it with a wire loop. Firm the soil and water the buried branch. When roots are well established, remove the layer from the parent plant and transplant it. Layering can be done in spring or summer. If it is done in late summer, the layered plants can be left over the winter and transplanted the following spring.

Division

Mint, French tarragon, and chives are commonly propagated by division, which is usually done in the spring before growth begins or at the end of the growing season. Dig up the old plant and cut or carefully pull it apart into sections. Each section is a new plant. Replant them and keep moist until established. Herbs that are propagated by division generally benefit from being dug up and divided every few years.

Harvesting and Drying Herbs

Harvesting

Small amounts of many fresh herbs can be harvested anytime during the growing season. Clipping leaves from the stem ends will encourage branching and bushier growth. Chives and parsley, though, should be cut from the base rather than the top. Do not harvest large quantities from woody herbs such as sage and thyme in late summer or fall. This would encourage new growth that does not have time to harden off before winter, and the plants will be more likely to experience winter injury.

Drying

Herbs from the garden can be dried for winter use and are often of better quality than store-bought herbs. Besides, what could look prettier in the kitchen than a big bouquet, wreath, or basket of dried herbs ready for use?

Herbs should be harvested for drying when they contain the maximum amount of essential oils, which provide the flavor and other desirable qualities. For leafy herbs this is usually when the flower bud just begins to open. Herb flowers, such as chamomile, are harvested just as they reach full flower. Seeds are harvested when they change from green to brown but before they drop.

Pick a dry, sunny morning after the dew has dried but before the sun is strong to harvest herbs. Remove seed heads and flowers unless you are drying the herbs for everlasting bouquets. If there is still some growing season left, cut leafy herbs only halfway down; they may make a second growth. In the fall, cut annuals to the ground.

The old-fashioned way to dry herbs is simply to hang them in bunches upside down in a dry, well-ventilated place out of direct light so they can retain as much color and essential oil as possible. Rinse them gently to remove any dirt and pick off dead or discolored leaves. When they are dry, the leaves can be stripped from the stems and stored in containers.

Short-stemmed herbs such as sweet woodruff, seeds, and flowers such as chamomile can be dried on a drying screen. Screens can be made of pieces of one-inch by two-inch lumber and window screening or cheesecloth, or you can use house window screens. (Serious herbalists often build special drying racks that hold many screens.) Strip the leaves or flowers from the stems and spread them in a thin layer on the screen. For very small-leafed herbs such as thyme, dry the whole stem. Place the screen in a warm, well-ventilated place out of direct sun. Gently stir and turn the leaves once a day.

A completely dried herb will powder easily when rubbed through the hands. If herbs are not completely dry to the touch, dry them in the oven for ten minutes at 200° F.

If drying seeds such as caraway, after about a week separate seeds from the capsule and stem, then place the seed and chaff in a pie tin. Blow over it while shaking the pan. The lighter chaff will blow away. Dry the seeds for an additional week or so before storing.

Some herbs, such as chives, parsley, borage, balm, chervil, and basil, do not dry well and should be frozen instead. Harvest and wash; pat dry. Strip the leaves and freeze them in small plastic bags or freezer boxes.

HERBS

I had a good clump of burdock under my study window and it was a great comfort, but the man would persist in cutting it down when he mowed the lawn. When I remonstrated, he declared that it was nothing but burdock; but I insisted that, so far from being burdock, it was really Lapa major, since which time the plant has enjoyed his utmost respect.

✸ LHB

ANGELICA *Umbelliferae family*

Angelica
(*Angelica archangelica*)

Angelica is the grande dame of the herb garden, reaching heights of five or six feet with its showy display of large, serrated leaves and greenish-white flowers in summer.

In the old herbals of Europe, angelica was known as a remedy for many ills, and it may be named after the Archangel Michael, the great protector, on whose feast day it was said to bloom. In medieval times it was thought to ward off plague.

Children knew angelica for its sweetness. The stem was crystallized to make candy or added to stewed fruits for extra sweetness.

The stems can be added fresh to salads or blanched and eaten like celery. The large, shiny leaves have the scent of sweet celery and can be cooked with fish, soups, and stews or made into a tea to ease colds and indigestion.

In addition to its usefulness, angelica is highly decorative, making a bold accent in shady areas of the garden and producing small but attractive flowers for fresh or dried arrangements.

Culture

Angelica is a biennial that grows as a basal rosette of leaves the first year and produces tall, flowering spikes the second. It can be made to grow a third season if the plants are kept from flowering, but the flowers are too pretty to pass up so most gardeners treat it as the biennial it is.

Angelica is grown easily from seed sown in late July and August as soon as seedheads ripen; seed viability decreases with age. It prefers partial shade and rich, moist, well-drained soil.

Archangel Michael

> I would preach the beauty of
> the common plants and the familiar places.
> These things are never old. ✷

Anise Hyssop *Labiatae family*

Anise Hyssop
(*Agastache foeniculum*)

The anise-flavored leaves of this member of the mint family add a tangy flavor to China and herb teas. The herb is a favorite with tea lovers and is also grown for the beauty of its small violet flowers, which bloom in dense, six-inch terminal spikes from early August through September.

Anise hyssop, sometimes known as Korean mint, is a lovely plant that makes an outstanding addition to any perennial border or herb garden. Its flowers are highly attractive to bees; thus the plant aids in garden pollination.

The leaves can be used dried or fresh to make a refreshing tea or combined with other teas to add an anise flavor. A few leaves in a fruit cup make a pleasant garnish. The leaves can also be added to potpourris and sachets for fragrance.

The flowers of this herb are edible and very tasty. Add them to salads, float them on soups, or use them to garnish meat dishes. They add color and fragrance to fresh bouquets and dry well, retaining both color and fragrance for a long time.

Culture

Anise hyssop is an erect perennial that reaches three or four feet in height. It can be grown from seed sown in spring or fall, and it self-sows vigorous volunteers that transplant easily. Or it can be increased by division in spring. Plants should be spaced twelve inches apart.

It likes rich soil and full sun but will tolerate light shade and is dense and hardy enough to be grown and trimmed as a short hedge, a technique favored by Victorian gardeners.

Herb Tea

A tea or herbal infusion is often the preferred way to use herbs. For each cup of water, place 1 teaspoon of dried leaves or 3 teaspoons of fresh leaves in a nonmetallic teapot. If using fresh leaves, slightly crush or bruise them before putting them in the pot to help release their flavor. Pour freshly boiled water over the leaves, stir once, then let steep for 5 to 10 minutes. A longer steeping time may give the tea a bitter taste; if the tea seems weak, increase the amount of leaves used, not the steeping time.

Other herbs traditionally used for tea are lovage, fennel, sage, mint, borage, lemon balm, and chamomile.

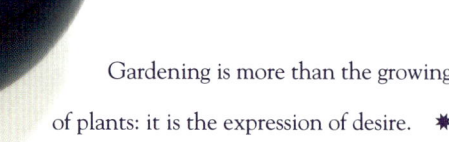

Gardening is more than the growing of plants: it is the expression of desire. ✸

Borage Boraginaceae family

Borage
(*Borago officinalis*)

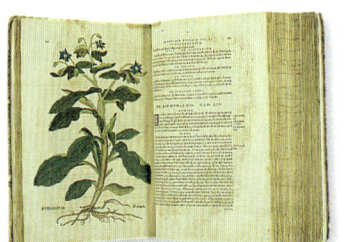

Borage as depicted by Leonhart Fuchs, in his 1542 herbal De Historia Stirpium, from the Rare and Manuscript Collection, Cornell University Library.

Borage is said to dispel sorrow and bring happiness, comfort, and courage. "Its use maketh a man merry and joyful," specified Pliny.

Native to Europe and northern Africa, borage can be easily grown outdoors in the garden and indoors in pots. A hardy annual, it grows up to two feet tall and produces beautiful blue star-shaped flowers. If the color looks familiar, it is because it is the sky blue chosen to represent the Madonna's robe in medieval art.

Although the blue flower is pretty enough to add to summer bouquets, borage is best known for its culinary attributes. The cucumber-flavored flowers are high in calcium, potassium, and mineral salts and can be added to salads or used as a pretty garnish. Like violets, they can be crystallized for cake decorations.

The young leaves can be chopped and added to sandwiches, cream cheese, and salads or dried and used for tea served hot or cold. Older, larger leaves can be cooked and eaten like spinach or batter-fried.

Medicinally, borage is useful for people who must follow salt-free diets because it is rich in mineral salts. Borage tea is said to stimulate the circulation and soothe the throat, and it has a mild diuretic effect. Applied externally, a poultice of leaves can reduce swelling and inflammation.

Culture

Borage is a hardy annual that grows rapidly and self-sows freely. Plant it in parts of the garden that have rich soil, plenty of sun, and are easy to maintain, making sure each plant has a minimum of two feet of space. Seed sown in the autumn will flower the following summer.

Bees are fond of borage, and the presence of a few plants will encourage them to visit the garden, resulting in better fruit set in the vegetable garden. Borage also makes a useful companion plant, deterring tomato worms and improving the growth and flavor of various vegetables.

May will shout with joy of new growths; July will nurture crop and tree; September will produce the seed after its kind. ✽

LHB

Caraway *(Carum carvi)*

If you want your love to stay true, feed him or her caraway seeds. They were once thought to possess the power of retention and were used to keep spouses, as well as livestock, from wandering.

The delicate, feathery leaves of caraway can be used in salads and soups, but cutting the foliage weakens the plant and jeopardizes your harvest of the prized aromatic seeds. Small, brown, and moon-shaped, the seeds are used to flavor rich meat dishes, soups, breads, cakes, apple pie, and cheese. Added to cabbage water, caraway reduces the strong smell of the vegetable.

Medicinally, caraway seeds aid digestion, promote appetite, and sweeten the breath, in addition to relieving flatulence. Caraway is an antispasmodic and is used to treat rheumatism and pleurisy.

A tea made by bruising caraway leaves is said to be stimulating and to relieve nausea. Powdered seeds can be put in poultices to ease bruises. Women have used caraway to regulate the menstrual cycle and induce lactation.

To test the browned seeds for ripeness before harvesting, gently pull a few from the largest flowerhead. If most pull away easily, cut the whole plant, turn it upside down in a large paper bag, and dry. Then roll the bag back and forth in your hands to loosen the seeds. Or dry the seeds in the sun for three days, bringing them in each night. Check to make sure there are no insects and store the seeds in jars. If they develop a musty smell, discard.

After the seeds have been harvested, the roots can be dug and cooked like carrots. The boiled roots are said to comfort a weak stomach.

Culture

Thankfully, considering its usefulness, caraway is relatively easy to grow in the home garden. Sow the seed directly in the garden in early spring (avoid transplanting, which it does not like), six to eight inches apart. Caraway likes full sun and well-drained soil. It will help loosen heavy soil so plant it abundantly. Caraway is a hardy biennial; plants grow to two feet.

Caraway Crackers

- 1 cup white flour
- 1 cup whole wheat flour
- 2 teaspoons caraway seeds
- ½ cup grated parmesan cheese
- 1 teaspoon salt (or to taste)
- 1 small onion, very finely minced
- 1 tablespoon oil
- Water to moisten (about ½ to ⅔ cup)

Combine the flours, seeds, cheese, and salt. Add onion and oil and enough water to make a stiff batter. Mix into a ball, roll out to ¼ inch on a floured board, cut into 2-inch rounds, and bake at 350 degrees till crisp and slightly brown, about 12 minutes. Makes about 2 dozen large crackers.

Chervil   *Umbelliferae family*

Chervil
(*Anthriscus cerefolium*)

Now widely known as a culinary herb, chervil, brought to Europe by the Romans, was once used to treat ills ranging from high blood pressure to senility. Its name, based on its warming properties, means "that which rejoices the heart." Pliny said that chervil would comfort the cold stomach of the aged; Evelyn instructed that every salad should contain some chervil to cheer the spirits.

It has been used as a spring tonic to cleanse the blood, to cure hiccups, to ease women's abdominal complaints, to expel kidney stones, and as a stimulant. Its leaves soothe bruises and rheumatism, and an infusion of chervil was thought to lower blood pressure.

In France, chervil is often substituted for parsley because the flavors are similar. Use the mild, slightly sweet leaves in salads, soups, and sauces and with vegetables, fish, egg, and chicken dishes. Because it is mild flavored, it can be used in greater quantity than some other herbs, almost like a green vegetable rather than a seasoning. Add the leaves toward the end of the cooking to retain their flavor. The stems can be chopped and added raw to salads.

The leaves can also be used to make a tea that aids digestion. Chervil is rich is vitamin C, carotene, iron, and magnesium.

Chervil does not dry well and is best used fresh. It can be frozen, however: combine one and a half cups of water and one cup of fresh chervil, whir through the blender, and freeze in covered ice cube trays.

Culture

Chervil is a hardy annual that requires light shade. Full sun will bleach out the delicate, fernlike foliage, which grows to fifteen inches. It starts easily from seed and will self-sow once established. (It needs light to germinate so don't cover the seeds with soil.) It is a good companion plant for radishes.

Because chervil germinates easily but does not transplant well, gardeners should plant the seed directly in the garden as soon as the soil can be worked. During spring and late summer the plant bears clusters of delicate, tiny, white flowers. If sown at three-week intervals over the summer and overwintered in a cold frame, chervil can be harvested year-round. It grows best in cold rather than hot weather.

Chervil Soup

3 tablespoons butter

3 tablespoons fresh, chopped chervil

3 tablespoons flour

4 cups hot vegetable stock or chicken broth

2 tablespoons heavy cream or half and half

Salt and pepper to taste

Heat the butter in a saucepan and gently sauté the chervil for 1 minute. Mix in the flour and stir till smooth. Add the stock or broth and simmer gently, covered, for 20 minutes. Just before serving, add the cream and salt and pepper to taste.

Serves 4.

CHIVES   *Amaryllidaceae family*

Chives
(*Allium schoenoprasum*)

Chives are the mildest-flavored member of the large and useful onion family.

Ancient herbalists and modern scientists alike agree that the alliums, including chives, garlic, and onions, have beneficial health properties, as well as adding a pleasant biting flavor to foods. They contain iron and vitamins and stimulate the appetite. Chives can be used abundantly in cooking because they usually do not cause the stomach upset sometimes associated with garlic and the larger onions.

Chives were used in China as long as four thousand years ago and now are found in many cuisines. The straight-growing, thin, cylindrical leaves, with their mild onion flavor, are used fresh or dried in meat, fish, egg, salad, soup, and vegetable dishes.

The bulbs can be dug and pickled like small onions or used to flavor sausage. The leaves can be frozen for winter use.

If the plants are divided regularly and harvested neatly, they are very attractive in the flower border or as an edging plant. They produce spiky, globular mauve flowers in early or midsummer. The flowers are edible and make pretty garnishes; to serve, pull them apart into individual florets.

Chives may help deter aphids and prevent mildew so some gardeners like to scatter them in clumps in rose beds.

Culture

The only difficulty with growing this hardy perennial is having enough friends to give clumps of chives to. The plant increases in size each year and also self-sows so gardeners eventually find themselves giving away as much as they harvest and still having plenty left in the garden. Divide the plants in spring or fall at least once every three years to keep them vigorous.

Chives like full sun and well-drained, moderately rich soil. If harvested frequently, they should be fertilized. They will grow in partial shade but will not flower as abundantly as they will in the sun.

Harvest the leaves by cutting at the base. After flowering, cut them back to about one inch to encourage a quick flush of new growth.

Chive Butter

For Flavoring Meats, Potatoes, and Sandwiches

Let ½ cup of butter soften to room temperature. Chop 1 teaspoon of fresh chives and mix into the butter with a little freshly ground pepper and the juice of one lemon. Shape in molds or put in crocks and chill until ready to serve.

Other herbs suitable for flavoring butter are thyme, sage, rosemary, parsley, dill, tarragon, and basil.

When one really feels the response to the native earth, one feels also the obligation and the impulse to share it with the neighbor. ✻ LHB

Clary Sage *Labiatae family*

Clary Sage
(*Salvia sclarea*)

Clary sage, also known as clear eye, a member of the mint family, makes a striking addition to the herb bed or perennial border. A fairly tall plant, it produces large white and purple bracts of flowers that remain showy even after they fade. The flowers smell pleasantly of spice and pine.

In addition to its handsomeness, this herb is useful. The leaves are good in omelets or fried in fritters. Cooked in stew, it will help tenderize tough meats, according to old herbals. Brewers can use clary to give beer a headier flavor, and wine made from the plant when it is in flower is said to be very pleasant and appealing.

Commercially, clary is grown for the oil that can be extracted from its leaves, which is used as a fixative in perfumes. At home, add dry clary leaves and flowers to sachets and potpourris.

Culture

Clary is a biennial that produces a basal rosette of leaves the first year and tall, handsome flowers the second. It can reach five feet in height and become greedy for garden space.

To have flowering plants each year, grow clary from seed sown in successive seasons. It will self-sow. It likes full sun and well-drained, average garden soil. In wet sites it will rot.

Clary Sage Fritters

4 tablespoons flour

6 tablespoons water

Pinch of salt

1 egg, separated

6 to 8 clary sage leaves

Vegetable oil

Mix the flour, water, and salt in a bowl. Beat the egg white till stiff in a separate bowl. Add the yolk to the flour mixture and beat. Gently fold egg white into the yolk mixture. Dip freshly picked clary sage leaves in the batter. Deep fry in vegetable oil till golden brown. Drain and serve.

Common Fennel — Umbelliferae family

Common Fennel
(Foeniculum vulgare)

Fennel, a relative of dill, has been a popular herb since biblical times, with many culinary and medicinal uses. All of this anise-flavored plant, from root to seed, is edible.

Fennel is often an ingredient in fish dishes and soups, and fennel seed is an appealing addition to sausages and baked goods.

A popular home remedy, fennel was used as a mild sedative, as an appetite stimulant, and by nursing mothers to aid milk production. Tea made with fennel is said to help in weight-loss programs. Like dill, fennel "comforteth the stomach," is an antiflatulent, and is good as an expectorant to ease chest colds.

If that isn't enough to recommend it for gardeners, warm compresses steeped in fennel tea are said to strengthen the eyes, and a facial pack of bruised fennel leaves may help prevent wrinkles.

In the garden, fennel's showy yellow flowers and fine foliage make an excellent background for smaller herbs and flowers.

Culture

Fennel is a fine-textured perennial that reaches four to five feet in height. The foliage is feathery and varies from lime green in spring to darker green in autumn. One variant, Copper, produces a gray foliage.

The herb produces golden-yellow, flat-topped umbels of flowers from mid-July to early September.

Fennel is commonly grown from seed and readily self-sows once established in the garden. Because of its taproot, fennel is difficult to transplant and should be sown where it is to grow. It likes full sun and average garden soil.

Var. *azoricum*, Florence fennel, is a smaller annual with a swollen, bulbous stem that can be harvested and eaten raw in salads or cooked.

Fennel Sauce

For Boiled or Baked Fish

½ cup butter

2 tablespoons fresh, chopped fennel leaves

Salt to taste

Melt the butter and add the fennel leaves and salt to taste. Pour warm over the cooked fish.

Or add 1 tablespoon fresh, chopped fennel to 1 cup of any basic white sauce.

COMMON WORMWOOD *Compositae family*

Common Wormwood
(*Artemisia absinthium*)

This delicately foliated, silver-gray herb is the bitter herb of biblical times. It was used in medieval England to wean nursing children. Early farmers used it to worm their cattle and themselves, hence its vulgar name. It was also used to make a liniment for aches and pains.

Commercially, wormwood provided the bitter flavor in the liqueur absinthe, which is toxic if consumed in large quantities, and vermouth.

Wormwood now is grown more for its historical interest and decorative value for than any household or culinary purpose. It produces small, yellow panicles of flowers in mid- to late summer, and the foliage, fresh or dried, is an excellent addition to arrangements.

Culture

Common wormwood is a wide-spreading woody perennial that reaches five feet in height. The finely cut leaves provide a gray accent in the perennial border or herb garden. Lambrook Silver is a lower-growing variant with particularly fine silver color.

It can be propagated by seed, which germinates slowly, stem cuttings, or division. Prune out the old wood at the base of the plant each spring. Staking may be necessary to keep the stems upright.

Wormwood prefers full sun and well-drained clay loam soil but will tolerate poor, dry soil and salt. It may do well in dry, sunny parts of the garden where moisture-loving plants will not thrive.

Coriander Umbelliferae family

Coriander (*Coriandrum sativum*)

A useful contact with the earth places man not as superior to nature but as a superior intelligence working in nature as a conscious and therefore as a responsible part in a plan of evolution, which is a continuing creation. ✸ LHB

And the house of Israel called the name thereof Manna; and it was like coriander seed, white; and the taste was like wafers made with honey.
—*Exodus 16:31*

Coriander is one of the oldest known herbs; references to it are found in the Bible, Sanskrit texts, and Egyptian papyri. In *Tales of the Arabian Nights* coriander is mentioned as an aphrodisiac, and the ancient Chinese believed it gave immortality.

All parts of the plant have culinary uses: leaves can be added to stews and sauces, the stem adds flavor to beans and soups, the root can be cooked like a vegetable, and the flavorful seeds are added to meat dishes and curries as well as apple pie. Coriander is a valuable herb used in Oriental, Indian, Mediterranean, Spanish, and Mexican cuisines.

The small, light-colored seeds have medicinal as well as culinary uses. They can be infused to make a digestive tonic, and they also have a mild sedative action. To improve appetite, chew the seeds or make a tea of them. Although the plant, especially the leaves, has a strong, almost pungent aroma, the dried seeds have a sweet, lemony flavor, which improves as they age. They are best kept for six months from time of harvest before using. Harvest the seeds after they have turned brown but before they drop.

Coriander leaves do not dry well but can be frozen for winter use.

Culture

Coriander is a hardy annual that grows to two feet. It prefers full sun and rich soil. Sow the seeds in early spring directly where the plants are to grow; thin the seedlings to eight inches apart.

Do not plant coriander near fennel; it will hinder the seed formation of fennel. It enhances the formation of anise seed and so makes a good companion planting for anise.

Dill   Umbelliferae family

Dill
(Anethum graveolens)

Dill is one of our oldest known herbs, dating back to biblical times and earlier. Egyptians found dill soothing, the ancient Greeks used this tall, feathery herb to cure hiccups, and medieval people used dill to fend off witchcraft. It has been used to soothe restless babies, hence its name from the old Saxon word *dillan,* to dull.

The early settlers of this country called it meeting seed and gave the seed to children to chew on during long sermons—it quieted hunger pangs.

We know dill mostly as a seasoning for soups, fish, and pickles. But the aromatic leaves, seeds, flowers, and stems of the plant can also be used to flavor cabbage, vinegars, apple pie, butter, cakes, and bread. Steeped in wine, dill is said to have mild aphrodisiacal qualities.

Medicinally, tea made from dill is said to ease digestion and help dispel flatulence; chewed seeds sweeten the breath. Dill is rich in minerals and is a good seasoning for low-salt meals. Women used dill to ease pains and problems of the womb, increase lactation, and make little cakes to comfort teething children.

To help retain the flavor in dried dill leaves, place them on paper in the shade for a day or two, then dry them completely in a warm oven. If drying time is prolonged, the leaves lose both color and flavor. The leaves can be preserved by freezing.

The seeds can be harvested as soon as the heads are brown and dry: gingerly cut the heads, trying to prevent the seed from scattering, and dry in a tray or on a sheet in the sun for four or five days. (Bring them in at night.) Finish drying in a warm oven, then store in glass jars away from direct light and heat.

Culture

Dill is a hardy annual that grows easily from seed and self-sows readily in moderately rich, loose soil. Sow seeds in the early spring in a sunny spot where the plants are to grow because they can be difficult to transplant. Make successive plantings from April through mid-July. The plants will grow from two to five feet tall. Leaves can be harvested as soon as eight weeks after seeding. Cut the outer leaves first, close to the stem. Use fresh or dried.

Don't plant dill close to fennel. The plants may cross-pollinate, affecting the flavor of the resulting seeds and leaves. Nor should dill be planted close to carrots. It is, though, an excellent companion crop for cabbage.

DITTANY OF CRETE   *Labiatae family*

Dittany of Crete
Origanum dictamnus
(Amaracus dictamnus)

Mentioned in Charlemagne's list of herbs, dittany was popular in medieval times as a medicinal and culinary herb. It was most often combined with other herbs such as rue and parsley to make a pepper sauce for fish or omelets.

The leaves were also used to make a healing tea.

Today, the thyme-scented herb is sometimes used to flavor salads, although this small, attractive plant is not as frequently grown as it deserves to be. It has trailing stems and gray-green, wooly foliage that adds interest to the rock garden, and it also makes an attractive indoor plant.

Culture

Dittany of Crete is a small, trailing perennial that is not hardy in the North. In cold climates it should be overwintered indoors.

Propagate by seed, stem cuttings, or divisions and grow in full sun and well-drained soil. It won't make a very large plant. Dittany is particularly attractive grown in hanging baskets.

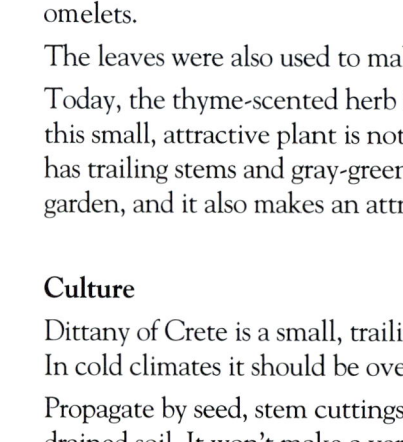

Like the love of music, books and pictures, the love of gardens comes with culture and leisure and with the ripening of the home life. ✻ LHB

FRENCH TARRAGON   *Compositae family*

French Tarragon
(*Artemisia dracunculus* 'French')

There are two kinds of tarragon, French and Russian, and they should not be confused. Russian tarragon is hardier, but it is the French tarragon that provides the unique flavor we associate with French cuisine.

The name of this herb, *dracunculus*, comes from the Latin for little dragon and may refer to its fiery, aniseed flavor or serpentine, gnarled roots. The herb was not overly popular in the Middle Ages but was recommended as a breath sweetener, sleep enhancer, and means of dulling the taste of bitter medicine. Tarragon leaves are a good source of mineral salts along with vitamins C and A.

French tarragon is an indispensable cooking herb that can be added to salads, sauces, soups, omelets, meats, and fish to give a mild anise flavoring.

This herb rarely flowers, and when it does the flowers are small, greenish, and insignificant. Nor is the plant particularly decorative. But it is a unique and important culinary herb. No bearnaise, hollandaise, or mousseline sauce would be complete without it.

Culture

French tarragon is a woody perennial that grows about two feet tall and has dark green, narrow, finely textured leaves. The plant does not produce seed and must be propagated by division or by stem cuttings in spring. Plant in full sun in rich, sandy, well-drained soil. Tarragon may tolerate poor, dry soil, but it most definitely will not tolerate the reverse. "Wet feet" may quickly kill this herb. Divide the plants every three or four years.

Vinegar

A quart jar with tight lid

Tarragon leaves

Rind of half a lemon: cut away as much white pith as possible

2 whole cloves

White vinegar

Filter papers

Small bottles with corks

Fill the jar with the fresh tarragon leaves and add the lemon rind cut in strips and cloves. Fill the jar with vinegar, cap tightly, and allow to stand in the sun for up to two weeks. Strain, pour through filter papers into small bottles, and cork tightly.

Garden Sage   *Labiatae family*

Garden Sage
(*Salvia officinalis*)

Sage was so highly thought of by early herbalists that they had a proverb to praise its usefulness: Why should a man die while sage grows in his garden? The ancient Greeks and many others believed sage to be a cure-all.

Sage was said to soothe the nerves, cure toothache, quiet the tremors of palsy, improve digestion, cure venom or poisoning, and ease itches. "Who that useth to eat of this herb or drink it, it is marvel that inconvenience should grieve them," *Bancke's Herbal* summarized.

Sage also played a role in early American history; it came to the rescue when the colonists boycotted English tea and needed homegrown substitutes.

Modern herbalists use sage leaves fresh or as a tea to treat head colds and sore throats, nervous headaches, and bad digestion.

Sage is one of the most popular culinary herbs, used to flavor everything from poultry to eggs to vegetables and fish. It is particularly good as a seasoning for meat, cutting the rich taste and making fatty foods easier to digest.

Culture

Garden sage is a shrubby perennial that grows to two and a half feet. It has square stems that are woody at the base and small, gray-green leaves. In June it produces small whorls of lavender flowers.

Variants: Albiflora produces white flowers and Tricolor has lower leaves with white margins and upper leaves tinged purple with pink. Tricolor is not reliably winter hardy. Aurea is compact and has leaves variegated with yellow; Purpurea has purple foliage.

Garden sage can be propagated by seed, stem cuttings, layering, and division; the variants should be grown by cutting, division, or layering. Sage likes full sun and moderately rich, well-drained soil. Give it an annual spring pruning to encourage bushy growth.

Sage is a perennial, but best results are secured by resowing every two or three years. ✴ LHB

Sage Sauce

For Roasted Meats

2 tablespoons butter

3 medium onions, chopped

2 tablespoons flour

2 cups beef bouillon

3 teaspoons fresh or 2 teaspoons dried sage leaves, very finely minced

½ cup half and half

Salt to taste

In a heavy skillet or saucepan, melt the butter and lightly sauté the chopped onions till soft and transparent, being careful not to burn them. Mix in the flour and cook, stirring until smooth. Add the bouillon and sage leaves and cook for about 1 minute, till sauce thickens. Slowly stir in the half and half. Salt to taste and serve spooned over sliced roasted meat or in a gravy bowl. Makes 3 cups.

Germander
(*Teucrium chamaedrys*)

This member of the mint family was once used to treat fevers, scurvy, asthma, and gout. Now, it's grown mostly for decoration and as a bee herb. Because it flowers from mid-July to mid-September, it provides nectar for bees for much of the growing season and is often planted near hives and in garden spots where pollination needs assistance.

Nearly evergreen, germander is a handsome plant that can be grown as a low hedge or edging in a formal garden. It has a pleasant, subtle mint fragrance and attractive small whorls of pink flowers on the upright stems.

The cultivar Prostratum grows to about eight inches in height and is an effective ground cover or rock garden plant.

Culture

Germander is a perennial that will grow one and a half feet tall if not clipped lower. Leaves are small, oval, and green for much of the year.

Germander can be grown from seed, but it is slow to germinate. It is more commonly propagated by stem cuttings, layering, or division. Germander grows in full sun or partial shade and well-drained, average garden soil.

HOREHOUND   *Labiatae family*

Horehound
(*Marrubium vulgare*)

Coughs have been treated with horehound for thousands of years. This bitter herb has been used medicinally since the ancient Egyptians called it "seed of Horus."

Horehound's small, heart-shaped leaves contain the essential oil, marrubium, which is prized as an expectorant and healer of bronchial conditions. They also contain significant quantities of vitamin C. To soothe a cough or a sore throat, finely mince nine small leaves from the plant and mix into one tablespoon of honey. Take as needed. For indigestion, pour one cup of boiling water over a few horehound leaves. Steep for five minutes, then strain out the leaves. Chill slightly before drinking.

This herb is a hardy perennial that grows about a foot and a half in height. After midsummer it forms clusters of small, white flowers that attract bees to the garden and also look pretty in delicate floral arrangements.

Harvest the leaves after the flower forms or anytime needed during the growing season. They can be used fresh or dried.

Culture

Horehound should be planted where it can enjoy full sun and protection from strong wind. It likes dry, alkaline soil and an annual spring pruning.

Horehound can be propagated by division, by taking stem cuttings, or by sowing seeds outdoors in late spring.

Horseradish *Cruciferae family*

Horseradish
(*Armoracia rusticana*)

Horseradish, also known as wild or mountain radish, great raifort, and red cole, is one of the bitter herbs eaten during Passover. Sinus sufferers should become familiar with this herb: one good whiff can open up a stuffy head.

Young horseradish leaves can be used in salads, but the plant is better known for its white, fleshy, pungent root, which is grated and eaten raw with meat or fish dishes. It can also be grated into coleslaw and mayonnaise-based sauces and dips. Horseradish, in addition to clearing the sinuses, is said to promote good digestion.

The fresh root contains calcium, sodium, magnesium, and enough vitamin C to help prevent scurvy. It also has antibiotic qualities. Heat destroys the volatile oils in horseradish so it should not be cooked. Applied as a plaster, horseradish root was used to treat sciatica, gout, and joint pains.

To harvest the roots, dig them in the fall and store in buckets of damp sand in a root cellar. Grate as needed and mix with vinegar for a simple sauce. Or leave the roots in the ground, mulch, and dig as needed. The root can be dried and then reconstituted with water.

Culture

Horseradish is a tough, medium-height perennial that most gardeners find more difficult to get rid of than to establish.

The plant develops no seeds and must be propagated through root cuttings. This is easy enough to do: make six-inch-long cuttings that include a bud from straight horseradish roots. Work the soil to a depth of two feet and then plant the cuttings a foot deep and a foot apart. Plant as early as possible, preferably in February, for a good fall crop. Locate the cuttings in a corner of the garden where only horseradish will be grown.

Hint: Horseradish growing near potatoes can deter potato bugs.

Horseradish prefers wet clay soil, supplemented with manure or compost, and a neutral pH of 7.0. To keep the long taproots growing straight, in the spring dig around the plants and remove the side roots. The plant grows to a height of two or three feet.

> ### Horseradish Sauce
>
> Peel and grate 4 tablespoons of horseradish root. Mix with 2 tablespoons oil, the juice of 2 lemons, and 2 minced garlic cloves. Add salt and pepper to taste.

The best roots are those planted in the spring at the time of setting early cabbage, and dug as late the same fall as the weather will permit. ✽ LHB

Hyssop   *Labiatae family*

Hyssop
(*Hyssopus officinalis*)

This semievergreen member of the mint family is grown today more for its decorative value than for medicinal or culinary purposes. It has a pleasant, spicy scent and produces lovely, deep blue-violet spikes of flowers from late June through August.

Hyssop grows thickly enough that it can be clipped to form a low hedge, and its semievergreen foliage provides color and interest in the winter garden. It makes an effective specimen plant in the perennial border, and the cut flowers are excellent in fresh floral arrangements. The flowers are edible and make an attractive garnish.

Earlier gardeners found the plant to be very useful as well as decorative. Its name may come from the Hebrew word *ezob*, for holy herb, because it was used to cleanse temples and lepers. Romans flavored wine with hyssop, and it is still used as a flavoring in the French liqueur Chartreuse. Very small amounts of slightly bitter, mint-flavored hyssop leaves can be added to salad, soups, and meat dishes. A poultice made from the leaves is reputed to be useful for treating insect bites.

Flowering hyssop will attract bees and butterflies to the garden. Grown near cabbages, it may help protect them from insect damage by luring away cabbage butterflies.

Culture

Hyssop is a perennial that grows to about two and a half feet. It has small, narrow, aromatic leaves. The spiky flowers are commonly a deep blue, but pink (Rosea) and white (Alba) varieties are also available.

Hyssop can be grown from seed sown in spring or fall or from division and stem cuttings. It likes full sun and light, well-drained, alkaline soil. Prune the plants back to several inches each spring to keep growth neat and attractive.

LADY'S MANTLE *Rosaceae family*

Lady's Mantle
(*Alchemilla vulgaris*)

Lady's mantle is probably so named because of its reputation as an herb particularly useful to women and because its leaves were believed to resemble the Virgin Mary's cloak. But its earlier Arabic name, *alkemelych*, "little magical one," reveals the anciently revered properties of this herb.

Its blue-green, almost circular, bitter-tasting leaves were used for a tea said to regulate menstrual periods, ease menopause, and prevent or heal problems of the female reproductive organs.

The leaves and stems can be used to make an infusion good for both skin tonic and mouthwash, and the root can be dug and used as a poultice to stop bleeding.

Lady's mantle, sometimes also known as dewcup, makes a very attractive plant in the garden. It grows as a low, bluish-green mound and from early June through July produces arching flower stems with small yellow clusters. The flowers are pretty in fresh bouquets and also dry well for winter arrangements.

Admire the plants in early morning before the diamondlike drops of dew that gather on each leaf evaporate.

Culture

Lady's mantle is an herbaceous perennial that grows about a foot tall. It will grow in full sun or partial shade and is decorative enough for the front of the perennial border and the rock garden, as well as the herb garden. It prefers rich, moist, alkaline soil.

Sow seeds or divide plants in spring or autumn, spacing the plants two feet apart.

Skin Tonic

Pour 1 cup of freshly boiled water over 3 teaspoons of fresh, bruised lady's mantle leaves. Steep for 5 minutes; strain and chill. Apply to face with cotton swabs. Leave on for 5 minutes, then rinse with lukewarm water.

Sage and peppermint also make refreshing skin tonics.

Lavender Cotton
Santolina chamaecyparissus (S. incana)

The herb known as lavender cotton is neither; it is actually a member of the daisy family.

Its foot-tall stems are woody and covered with small, fine-toothed, silver-gray leaves that give off a pungent scent of camphor and resin. From late June to mid-July the plant produces small, buttonlike yellow flowers.

Lavender cotton is an excellent, compact, silvery-gray accent plant for the foreground of the perennial border or rock garden. It does not flower abundantly, and many gardeners remove the flowers so they don't distract from the lovely foliage.

Lavender cotton can be clipped to form a low hedge and is popular in knot gardens and formal herb gardens.

The flowers can be added to dried arrangements or potpourris, and branches of the herb can be put into drawers and closets to discourage moths.

Santolina virens, green santolina, is similar to lavender cotton but has bright green foliage and numerous yellow, buttonlike flowers.

Culture

Lavender cotton is a nearly evergreen perennial of medium height. It is attractive as an accent plant or grown as a low hedge in the rock garden or perennial border.

Lavender cotton can be grown from seed, which is slow to germinate, or propagated by stem cuttings, layering, or division. It prefers full sun and light, moderately rich, well-drained soil. It will tolerate salt and dry soil.

Prune lightly in the spring and give the protection of a winter mulch in cold climates.

Particularly it is good to celebrate the yearly bounty. ✸ LHB

Lemon Balm (*Melissa officinalis*)

Labiatae family

If lemon balm leaves smell familiar when crushed, it's because this lemon-scented member of the mint family has long been a valued addition to perfumes, liqueurs, and furniture polish.

Perhaps we should grow more accustomed to its taste than its smell: people have claimed to have lived to be one hundred years old because of drinking lemon balm tea daily! This herb was said to renew youth and dispel melancholy. Today, herbalists recommend lemon balm tea for relief from coughs, colds, and headaches.

In addition to making a fragrant, invigorating tea, lemon balm can be used in cooking to flavor salad, soup, stew, fish, poultry, vegetables, and meat.

Chop the oval, hairy leaves fine for fresh use. Their flavor is best just when the plant's small, white flowers begin to open in mid-July. Leaves may be dried for winter use. They are so aromatic they make a good addition to potpourris and herbal pillows.

In the garden, lemon balm grows as an attractive mound that serves as a fragrant filler and background for smaller plants.

Culture

Lemon balm is a hardy herbaceous perennial that grows up to three feet tall. It prefers full sun but will tolerate some shade.

It can be grown from seed sown in spring or divisions and stem cuttings in spring and fall. Space plants two feet apart and cut them back when they finish flowering in September.

A variety of lemon balm, Aurea, has pretty, variegated green and gold leaves in spring and autumn.

The best understanding of our relations to the earth will be possible when we learn how to apply our devotions in the open places. ❋ LHB

Lemon Verbena
Aloysia triphylla
(Lippia citriodora)

The leaves of this deciduous, woody shrub have a sharp lemon fragrance that is used in perfumes, soaps, and cosmetics. Home gardeners enjoy adding the dried leaves to potpourris and herb pillows.

Lemon verbena originated in South America. It is popular in Spain as a tea herb; it has a reputation for producing a calming, sedative effect. Young leaves can be used in fruit drinks, salads, and jellies and as a substitute for lemon rind.

Culture

Lemon verbena is not hardy in the North and should be overwintered indoors, especially in cold climates. It is often grown as a patio or pot plant.

If grown outdoors during the summer, it will lose its leaves when brought inside. Give the plant a rest and water sparingly. New growth will begin in late winter, at which time it should be pruned. If pot grown, the shrub can reach five feet in height. In late summer or autumn it produces slender spikes of small, pale flowers.

Lemon verbena can be propagated by stem cuttings taken in summer or grown from seed.

Herb Pillow

Herb pillows are an old-fashioned method of treating insomnia. They are made of dried herbs sewn into a pillow made of loose, porous material that allows the scent of the herbs to escape.

Dry the leaves or flowers of herbs thought to have a calming effect for your sleep pillow. Lavender, lemon balm, woodruff, rosemary, and lemon verbena are some of the commonly used ones. Mix the herbs to achieve a pleasing fragrance.

Lovage
(*Levisticum officinale*)

Accommodating lovage will grow just about anywhere in the garden, but don't plant more than a few of these tough perennials. Each plant may grow up to six feet tall and five feet wide.

Its nickname, love parsley, indicates one of the traditional uses of this herb: as a love potion. In Europe it was known as a love charm and an aphrodisiac. Travelers put leaves of it in their shoes to cool and deodorize their feet. Cordials flavored with lovage and tansy were also popular with travelers.

Modern herbalists may grow lovage because it is so handsome in the garden and adaptable in the kitchen. The large, celery-flavored leaves can be used to flavor soup, stew, cheese, and chicken dishes. Small, young leaves can be added to salads, and the root can be dug, peeled, and cooked or candied.

Seeds are good in breads, herb butters, meat loaf, and cakes, but check the seed heads for aphids, which are attracted to this plant, before harvesting.

A tea made from the leaves, fresh or dried, aids digestion and is a mild diuretic. Added to bath water or placed directly on wounds, the herb is both antiseptic and antibiotic. The seeds when chewed relieve flatulence.

The leaves can be harvested all summer long for using fresh, but they are somewhat difficult to dry. They must be dried quickly and out of bright light. Spread the leaves on screens in single layers and finish drying in a warm oven. Cool, bottle, and use within a year. Or purée the leaves with a little water and freeze in ice cube trays.

Culture

This useful, hardy perennial is easy to grow. Sow the seeds in late summer and in the autumn transplant the seedlings to their permanent location in either full or partial sun. (They can also be sown in spring.)

Avoid places that are excessively dry and those with poor drainage. After four years the plants may need to be divided to keep them vigorous. Division should be done in the spring, when the first shoots push through the soil. For best results, fertilize heavily with manure, compost, and lime. Cut off old, yellowing leaves and harvest young leaves and stalks frequently to encourage new growth.

Lovage needs a period of dormancy so in warmer climates it should be grown as an annual.

In addition to being one of the larger plants in the herb bed, lovage is one of the longer-lived ones, thriving twenty years and longer with care.

MINT *Labiatae family*

Mint
(*Mentha*)

Mintho, the beautiful nymph who gave her name to this herb, was loved by Pluto, god of the underworld. Persephone, who had already been abducted by Pluto, grew jealous of Mintho and turned her into a fragrant, lovely plant, which to this day waits at the shady edges of Pluto's dark realm. Or so said the ancient Greeks.

This herb has been beloved and used for time immemorial. Mints were so important to biblical peoples that they were accepted as payment of taxes. They were also used as culinary, medicinal, and strewing herbs. (Long before carpets became common, fragrant and pungent herbs were strewn over bare floors to absorb spills, sweeten the air, and discourage insects and mice. Strewing herbs are still useful in linen cupboards, closets, and kitchen drawers.)

Peppermint
(*Mentha x piperita*)

This popular herb is used to flavor everything from chewing gum to medicine. It grows easily, even invasively, in the home herb garden and is most frequently used to make a cooling, chilled summer tea.

An ancient, forgotten purpose for peppermint was to use the leaves to scour and clean wooden tables: it left behind a clean, fresh scent that helped the appetite. A peppermint-scoured table was considered a mark of hospitality.

Culture

Peppermint is an herbaceous perennial that grows to three feet in height. The square stems often have a purple tinge. Many gardeners restrict it to naturalistic areas near water or a separate bed because it has invasive rhizomes and is not of ornamental value.

Peppermint will grow in full sun or partial shade in moist but well-drained soil and can be propagated by division, stem cuttings, root cuttings, and layering. It benefits from an annual root pruning.

Poached Pears

2 ½ cups water

1 cup sugar

1 cup loosely packed fresh mint leaves (reserve a few leaves for garnishing)

4 pears

Sweetened whipped cream (optional)

Combine the water, sugar, and mint in a saucepan large enough to hold the pears and bring to a boil. Simmer for 10 minutes, stirring occasionally, then strain the mint leaves from the syrup.

Peel the pears (you may leave strips of peel for a decorative effect) and simmer them in the syrup for 10 to 20 minutes, or until a fork easily pierces the flesh. (Cooking time will depend on how ripe the pears are.) Carefully turn the pears several times while they cook. Chill them in the syrup for several hours, preferably overnight.

To serve, put pears on individual dessert plates, spoon a little syrup over each, and garnish with fresh mint leaves. Can be accompanied by sweetened whipped cream if desired. Serves 4. This recipe can be doubled or tripled.

Pineapple mint

MINT *Labiatae family*

Corsican Mint
(*Mentha requienii*)

This small, low-growing mint is attractive in the rock garden, with other small-scale plants, or near a small garden pool. It also makes a decorative and fragrant house plant. Like other mints, it can be used to flavor iced drinks and fruit cups.

Culture

A low, creeping perennial that grows to about an inch in height, Corsican mint is not always hardy in the North. It needs protection in the winter or should be overwintered indoors.

It can be grown from seed or division and self-sows to some extent. It will grow in full sun or partial shade, in moist, well-drained soil.

Spearmint
(*Mentha spicata*)

This is the mint most commonly used for garnishing iced tea and mint juleps and for flavoring mint sauces, mint jelly, and vinegar. Small quantities of finely minced fresh leaves can also be added to fruit salads and peas.

A hot tea made from spearmint is said to relieve nausea, induce sweating in high fevers, and act as a restorative. The ancients added spearmint to their food to lift the spirits and prevent melancholy.

Culture

Spearmint is an herbaceous perennial that reaches two and a half feet tall. Like peppermint, it has invasive rhizomes and is often grown in naturalistic areas or a separate bed.

Propagate by division, stem cuttings, or root cuttings rather than seed because germination is erratic. It will take full sun or partial shade with moist, fertile soil. Divide every three or four years.

PARSLEY *Umbelliferae family*

Parsley
(*Petroselinum crispum*)

There's a good reason why parsley is the most common garnish in Western cuisine. It cleans the breath, aids digestion, and prevents flatulence. So don't push it off to the side the next time it adorns your plate; save it as the last tasty mouthful of the meal and enjoy its benefits.

The ancient Romans believed parsley to be a fertility aid, a guard against intoxication, and a diuretic that helps prevent kidney stones. Herbalists through the ages have praised the health-supporting qualities of this herb.

Modern scientists know that parsley is rich in calcium, iron, thiamin, riboflavin, niacin, vitamin A, and vitamin C.

But parsley also has a dark side: in some mythologies, it was identified with death and the underworld, possibly because it takes so long to germinate. Early Christians claimed that parsley had to go to the devil and back seven times before it would sprout.

In the kitchen, parsley, both the flat and curly-leaved varieties, is indispensable both as an edible garnish and as a flavoring. Parsley can be used fresh, dried, or frozen and thawed in salads, stews, soups, sauces, and salad dressings. Parsley leaves make a rich tea high in vitamin C, and the seeds make a tea that is good for asthma and menstrual problems.

Pick the older leaves before the younger ones or cut the whole plant to one inch above the ground, being careful not to damage the growing point.

Culture

Low-growing and leafy, parsley makes a handsome edging plant in either flower or vegetable garden. It likes full sun and rich, well-drained soil.

To grow parsley from seed, start with fresh seed (old will not germinate) and soak it in warm water for twenty-four hours. Plant in early spring, spacing twelve inches apart. In areas where summer temperatures exceed 90 degrees for prolonged periods, parsley can be sown in the fall for early spring harvest next year.

It can also be started indoors in the winter; if the seedlings must be transplanted, do so before a full crown of leaves has developed. Or sow the seed directly into pots in midsummer and bring the pots indoors over the winter. They'll need a bright sunny window.

Parsley is a biennial that will self-sow the second summer, but most gardeners treat it as an annual.

Persillade Sauce

2 hard-boiled eggs

6 tablespoons Italian salad dressing

½ to ⅔ cup fresh, chopped parsley

Chop the eggs into fine pieces and mix with the dressing and parsley. Let stand 15 minutes before serving so flavors can mix. The sauce is good with cold meats.

Roman Chamomile
Chamaemelum nobile
(Anthemis nobilis)

An old proverb describes the hardiness of this sunny herb: "Like a chamomile bed, the more it is trodden the more it will spread." English gardeners used to plant entire lawns of chamomile, and medieval herbalists planted the small, daisylike herb on paths and benches, where it would release a pleasant apple scent when walked or sat upon.

Dried flowers of chamomile have been used to make tea for centuries; it is a sedative and useful for fighting colds and fevers. Early herbals recommended it as a treatment for headache, liver problems, and gallstones.

Chamomile has been used in many ways as a cosmetic herb and was a favorite with women, who always reserved a place for it in the garden. Adding chamomile flowers to the bath water will help relieve chapped, sunburned skin. Rinsing hair with chamomile brings out highlights in blond hair, and a compress soaked in warm chamomile tea relieves red and swollen eyes.

Both the flower and the finely cut leaves can be dried and added to potpourris and herb pillows. Harvest the flowers just as the white petals begin to bend back.

The delicate flowers are pretty in fresh arrangements and can be added to finger bowls to sweeten the water.

Culture

Roman chamomile is a mat-forming perennial that grows two to four inches tall. The leaves are bright green and very finely cut. The small yellow and white daisylike flowers are borne on upright ten-inch stems from mid-June to mid-August.

Chamomile can be grown from seed, division, or stem cuttings. It likes full sun and a light, dry soil. The plants can be invasive and need to be kept in bounds with periodic pruning. If you have a spot in the garden where the ground does not freeze for long periods, try growing chamomile as a turf in place of grass. It makes a good ground cover in sunny spots.

Rosemary Labiatae family

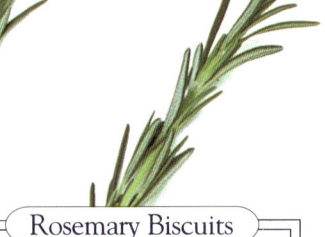

Rosemary
(*Rosmarinus officinalis*)

"There's rosemary, that's for remembrance," Ophelia tells Laertes. He was probably already well aware of that: rosemary has long been known as a memory strengthener and hence as a symbol of remembrance. The Elizabethans considered rosemary a symbol of constancy and used it at both weddings and funerals as a token of remembrance.

Old legends say that this herb will never grow more than six feet in height, which was supposedly Christ's stature, and that the delicate blue color of the flowers is in homage to the Virgin, who draped her cloak over a rosemary bush during the flight from Egypt.

One of the stranger customs associated with this herb was the medieval English belief that rosemary growing outside a door meant the wife within was the boss: husbands sneaked out at night to dig up the plant! In France, young women combed their hair with rosemary to prevent giddiness.

Its name most likely is from the Latin *ros*, dew, and *marinus*, the sea, because the herb's native habitat was among the misty hills of the Mediterranean seaside.

The delicate, needlelike leaves of rosemary are used to flavor lamb, pork, poultry, beef, veal, stew, stuffing, vegetables, herb butters, vinegars, jam, and herb bread.

A tea made from rosemary leaves is reputed to ease headaches and improve circulation.

Culture

Rosemary is an evergreen perennial that will grow up to six feet tall in warm climates. In the North, it must be overwintered indoors. It has erect, woody stems and short, needlelike leaves with a spicy pine scent.

The seed is slow to germinate, and the plant is most commonly propagated from stem cuttings, division, or layering. It grows in full sun and rather dry, alkaline soil. Indoors, give it a cool, sunny, humid location.

Variants: Albus has white flowers rather than blue; Collingwood Ingram has graceful, curving stems; Lockwood de Fores has prostrate stems and light green leaves; Tuscan Blue has blue-violet flowers.

Rosemary Biscuits

2 cups flour

2 teaspoons baking powder

Pinch of salt

1 teaspoon sugar

1 teaspoon dried ground rosemary leaves

4 tablespoons butter

⅔ cup milk

1 egg

Sift together the flour, baking powder, salt, sugar, and rosemary. Work in the butter till flour mixture resembles coarse meal. Mix together the milk and egg and add to flour mixture. Mix with fork till dough leaves the side of the bowl, then knead lightly and briefly on a floured board. Roll out to half-inch thickness, cut into 2-inch rounds, and bake at 450 degrees for about 12 minutes, or until lightly browned. Makes about 18 biscuits.

Rue *Rutaceae family*

Rue
(*Ruta graveolens*)

Bitter rue was known in medieval times as the herb of grace, useful for warding off plague, witches, bugs, and headache. On Midsummer Eve, maidens gathered rue and rose, St. John's wort, and vervain to make a green "Midsummer Man" to divine whether their lovers were true.

Pseudo-Apuleius recommended a compress of rue soaked in vinegar and applied to the forehead to ward off lethargy and forgetfulness. *Bancke's Herbal* recommends it as a specific for spleen and liver problems and feebleness of sight.

If rue leaves look slightly familiar, that's because the suit of clubs in playing cards is the same shape.

Today, rue is grown most often as a decorative plant. It has delicate, rounded, blue-green leaves that make a nice accent in the perennial border. Semievergreen, it provides garden color for much of the year, and it can be clipped into a low hedge for knot gardens.

Very small quantities of the fresh, bitter leaves can be chopped and added to salads or sandwiches or to flavor vinegar. English country women used rue tea to treat dizziness and female disorders.

Rue is also useful as a bug deterrent: hang bunches of it in windows to discourage flies.

Culture

Rue is a shrubby perennial that grows to three feet in height. The leaves are small and blue-green, and the erect stems bear yellow flower clusters from mid-June through August.

Variants include Blue Beauty with bright blue-green leaves, Blue Mound, which grows more compactly, Jackman's Blue, which has the strongest blue color of all the variants, and Variegata, whose leaves are variegated with white.

Rue can be grown from seed, but variants must be propagated from stem cuttings or division. It likes full sun and well-drained clay loam soil. It will tolerate poor soil and some light shade.

Use caution when handling rue. Some people are allergic to the oil in the plant and may develop a rash.

SALAD BURNET   *Rosaceae family*

Salad Burnet
Poterium sanguisorba (Sanguisorba minor)

Salad burnet is one of the herbs brought to the New World by the Pilgrims, who cherished it for its ability to "make the heart merry."

Its Latin name is from the Greek word for drinking cup, *poterion*, and salad burnet was often mixed with wine and other beverages. Poultices of crushed leaves were used to stop bleeding.

It is a tough perennial that grows easily from seed and has green leaves for much of the year. The leaves are very high in vitamin C throughout the plant's long growing season. No wonder the early colonists thought so highly of this valuable herb.

The young leaves have a delicate cucumber flavor that is refreshing in a salad or as a flavoring for vinegar. They can also be used to flavor butter or cream cheese and as a garnish.

Culture

Salad burnet is a perennial that grows as a compact, foot-tall mound with lacy foliage handsome enough for the front of the border. It produces feathery, reddish-purple, oblong flowerheads from late May to mid-June. In a mild winter, leaves near the ground will stay green.

Grow from seed or division in spring. It likes full sun and well-drained garden soil but will tolerate poor, dry soil.

Remove the flowers to retain the compact growth habit of the plant.

SCENTED GERANIUM *Geraniaceae family*

Scented Geranium
(*Pelargonium*)

Most gardeners are familiar with large-flowering geraniums, but there are also many scented geraniums that produce small flowers with marvelous fragrances.

These scented geraniums are excellent additions to potpourris and sachets and for fragrant teas and jellies. Or add a small piece of fresh leaf to flavor custard.

Colonial cookbooks recommended lining pound cake pans with scented geranium leaves, especially rose geranium, before pouring in the batter. Bake as the recipe requires, then turn the cake out of the pan and gently remove the leaves before serving.

For a pleasant fragrance, add a few scented geranium leaves to the sugar bowl.

Lemon Geranium
(*Pelargonium crispum*)

As its name states, this geranium has a lemon-scented foliage. It grows in a narrow, erect form to three feet in height and has small leaves and small, pink flowers.

Rose Geranium
(*Pelargonium graveolens*)

The rose-scented geranium grows to three feet in height and has handsome, deeply lobed foliage. It makes a fragrant bedding or container plant. Popular variants include Grey Lady Plymouth, with its silver foliage, Red-flowered Rose, which is compact with cerise flowers, and Rober's Lemon Rose, which has a lemon-rose scent and delicate pink flowers.

Geranium Tea

Take about 1 teaspoon of fresh or dried leaf from one of the scented geraniums, crush, and put in the bottom of a teacup. Cover with boiling water and let steep for a few minutes. Sweeten to taste. Serve hot or chilled.

Every family can have a garden.
If there is not a foot of land, there are porches or windows.
Wherever there is sunlight, plants may be made to grow. ✷ LHB

SCENTED GERANIUM *Geraniaceae family*

Apple Geranium
(*Pelargonium odoratissimum*)

A larger-leafed variety, the apple geranium has short, woody stems, numerous trailing branches, and a sweet apple fragrance. Its trailing habit and white umbels of flowers make this geranium particularly handsome in a hanging basket. The apple geranium produces abundant seed and can be grown from seed.

Peppermint Geranium
(*Pelargonium tomentosum*)

Growing one to two feet tall, the peppermint-scented geranium produces large, hairy leaves with a strong mint scent. Wide-spreading, it requires ample space in the garden and will grow in light shade or full sun.

Culture

Geraniums are herbaceous perennials that are not hardy in the North. They are grown as annuals or as pot plants and can be overwintered indoors. Cuttings or the entire plant can be brought inside, but cut plants back or they will get very leggy and scraggly.

Most geraniums can be propagated by stem cuttings. Grow them in full sun in moist soil and regularly pinch off terminal shoots to encourage branching.

Scented Geranium Jelly

To any basic recipe for apple jelly, add 1 finely chopped, medium-sized geranium leaf for each cup of liquid before adding the sugar called for in the recipe. Make jelly according to recipe. Strain out leaf when pouring into jars, or leave in to provide color.

This jelly makes an interesting companion to roast meats, lamb, or chicken.

Other herbs suitable for flavoring jelly are mint, bay, sage, tarragon, and thyme.

Peppermint geranium

Southernwood *Compositae family*

Southernwood
(*Artemisia abrotanum*)

This pungent herb's nickname, lad's love, attests to its ancient reputation as an aphrodisiac. It was said to cause intense desire simply lying under the pillow; canny lads added it to bouquets they gave their sweethearts. More modest sources say the herb earned its name by causing the beard to grow thicker when young men rubbed it on their faces.

Strangely enough, southernwood's genus, *Artemisia*, comes from the Greeks, who named it in honor of Artemis, the goddess of chastity. The Greek word *abros*, delicate, refers to the finely cut shape of the leaves.

Although the feathery leaves can be used to make a stimulating, antiseptic tea, southernwood is better known for its domestic rather than medicinal uses.

Its fruity, lemon fragrance is pleasant added to sachets and potpourris and is said to repel moths. Hanging a bunch of southernwood in open windows may discourage flies.

Southernwood is prized in the herb garden, not for the small, yellowish-white flowers it produces in August but for its very finely divided foliage, which contrasts well with many other plants, and its lemony fragrance.

Culture

Southernwood is a woody perennial that grows as a clump, often up to four feet tall. In good conditions it will grow densely enough that it can be clipped as a low hedge.

It prefers full sun and well-drained, average garden soil. It does not tolerate poor, dry soil.

Propagate by division in spring or fall and by stem cuttings. Cut the plants back in spring to remove old wood.

Summer Savory *Labiatae family*

Summer Savory
(*Satureja hortensis*)

Summer savory, whose name recalls satyrs, or satureja, has been an important culinary and medicinal herb for two thousand years.

A stimulant, summer savory was long believed to be an aphrodisiac, which may explain why it was named after the mythic and very affectionate satyrs.

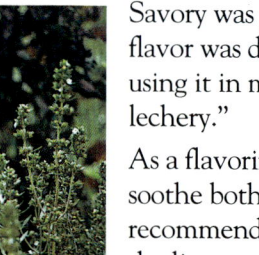

Savory was popular in dishes in which a mild pepper flavor was desired, but *Bancke's Herbal* advised against using it in meat dishes because it "stirreth him that useth lechery."

As a flavoring for wine, summer savory was thought to soothe both the nerves and stomach, and early herbalists recommended it as a purgative and a remedy for ills of the liver and lungs. Women used a skin tonic of summer savory to whiten their complexions. Crushed leaves of summer savory can relieve the pain of bee stings.

In Germany this herb is known as *Bohnenkraut*, or bean herb, because it is commonly cooked with beans and meat—and for good reason. Adding summer savory to gaseous foods such as beans and cabbage can help reduce the flatulence they produce.

Culture

Summer savory is a bushy, compact annual that grows about a foot and a half tall. It has small whorls of lilac-pink flowers from midsummer to frost and bronze-purple leaves in late summer.

To keep the leaves plentiful for harvest, cut back the flower heads as soon as they appear.

Summer savory grows easily from seed and will self-sow to some extent. Transplant or sow directly where the plants are to grow as soon as the ground can be worked. Plant in full sun, in average garden soil. The plants become top-heavy, but if placed close together for support and with the stems hilled up with soil, they probably won't need to be staked. Keep them moist during dry weather.

In the vegetable garden, summer savory can be grown as a companion plant with beans and onions. It will improve their growth and flavor and will deter bean beetles.

Summer savory can be grown indoors in a pot. The plants should be misted twice a week and kept moist.

Sauce for Poultry

2 tablespoons oil

1 cup sliced mushrooms

1 tablespoon each of fresh, finely chopped summer savory and parsley

2 tablespoons flour

1½ cups chicken broth

½ cup white wine

Salt and pepper to taste

3 tablespoons sour cream

Heat the oil and sauté the mushrooms and herbs. Add the flour and cook, stirring until smooth. Add chicken broth, wine, and salt and pepper to taste and stir until sauce thickens. Cook over medium to low heat, covered, for 15 minutes. Add the sour cream just before serving. Pour over cooked poultry (shown here over baked chicken breasts). Makes enough to accompany 4 servings.

Sweet Basil *Labiatae family*

Sweet Basil
(*Ocimum basilicum*)

Pesto Genovese

2 cups fresh basil leaves

⅓ cup olive oil

3 cloves garlic, peeled and minced

1 tablespoon pine nuts

¼ teaspoon salt

½ cup grated parmesan cheese

Put the basil, oil, garlic, pine nuts, and salt in a blender and process till smooth. Stir in the cheese. Toss with 1 pound cooked pasta. Makes four servings.

To keep your home safe from harm, plant plenty of basil around it. So says one of the many legends about this herb. Known to the Greeks as *basilion* (royal herb) and the Italians as *bacia-nicola* (Kiss-me-Nicholas), it symbolizes courtship, sanctity, and good wishes.

One of the more amusing legends about basil is that it must be sown amid vile shouts and curses if it is to thrive. The French have an idiom, *semer la basilic*, or sowing the basil, which means to rant and rave. Perhaps all this letting off of steam is why the plant protects the home after it has been sown. Contemporary gardeners have been known to grow basil successfully without flamboyant sowing displays.

With its mild, clovelike scent and flavor, basil is indispensable in the kitchen for flavoring soups, stews, and sausages. Mediterranean cuisine especially makes generous use of basil; it's the main ingredient in Pesto Genovese.

Basil can also be used to flavor vinegars. Dark opal basil, infused in vinegar, imparts an attractive color and added flavor. *Ocimum basilicum* Citriodorum, or lemon-scented basil, can be used to make a spicy, lemon-flavored tea that dispels nausea.

Medicinally, basil has been used for nervous disorders, stomach cramps, whooping cough, and headache. It has antispasmodic and antibacterial qualities, along with a mild sedative action.

Culture

Basil is a good companion plant for tomatoes, helping to protect them from disease and insects. It's also a good herb to plant near your outdoor living areas because it repels flies and mosquitoes.

Basil is an annual that should be grown in full sun, in enriched, well-drained soil, and with protection from cold winds.

Start the seeds indoors and don't transplant into the garden until both days and nights are warm. Or sow directly into the garden after all danger of frost has passed. Plant twelve inches apart and regularly pinch the tops to encourage branching.

Lemon basil should be sown directly in the garden, six inches apart. It can be transplanted, but directly sown plants will be more robust.

Keep the soil weed-free, well aerated, and supplemented with rotted manure. Basil also grows well in pots, and in the fall plants can be lifted from the soil and potted and grown indoors.

The leaves can be harvested at any time and used fresh, dried, or frozen.

Sweet Cicely *Umbelliferae family*

Sweet Cicely/Myrrh
(*Myrrhis odorata*)

Sweet cicely's fernlike foliage and lacy white flowers are so attractive that this herb can be grown as a foundation plant on the north side of the house. Handsome in the garden, it is indispensable in the kitchen.

It has been a popular herb throughout history and was especially popular in Elizabethan times, when it was valued for its sweet, aniselike flavor.

Contemporary cooks can add sweet cicely to fruit pies and reduce the amount of sugar needed.

Or add the finely minced leaves to salad dressings, omelets, soups, stews, herb butters, cooked root vegetables, fruit cups, and whipped cream. It will improve any dish that benefits from a mild, sweet, anise flavoring.

The roots can be used like parsnips, and the seeds go well in candy, syrups, cakes, and liqueurs.

Like many early spring herbs, sweet cicely is considered a tonic that strengthens and restores and is especially good for the digestion.

Culture

Sweet cicely is one of the more attractive herbs with its deeply cut foliage and umbels of white spring flowers. It is also one of the first plants to come up in spring and continues until late in the season.

It is a thick-rooted perennial that grows to three feet in height. If grown from seed, sow the seed in the fall because freezing promotes its germination. Or propagate by division in the fall.

Sweet cicely likes partial shade and moist, well-drained soil. Plants take several years to reach mature sizes.

Plum Salad

1 pound ripe plums

1 tablespoon fresh sweet cicely, chopped

½ cup yogurt

Juice of half a lemon

Stone and dice the plums, add the chopped sweet cicely, and mix in the yogurt and lemon juice. Chill and serve.

Sweet Marjoram   *Labiatae family*

Sweet Marjoram
Origanum majorana
(Majorana hortensis)

Origanum is from the Greek *oros ganos*, or joy of the mountain, which aptly describes marjoram's sweet and spicy scent. It's one of our oldest herbs, favored by the ancient Egyptians and Greeks and in use in Europe since the Middle Ages.

The ancient Greeks massaged themselves with sweet marjoram oil to refresh and heal themselves, and the herbalist Culpepper said that this herb would strengthen the stomach and head, restore appetite, ease cough and consumption of the lung, and prevent dropsy, scurvy, scabs, and itch.

To ease aches, pains, and stiff joints, tie a handful of marjoram leaves in a muslin bag and add it to your bath. If insomnia is a problem, put a muslin bag of bruised leaves in your pillow case. For thinning hair, try massaging oil of marjoram into the scalp.

As useful as this herb is in the medicine cabinet, though, we are more familiar with wild marjoram's indispensability in the kitchen, where it traditionally flavors Italian specialties from tomato sauces to egg dishes. Fresh leaves can be chopped fine and added to salads, sauces, pizza, and meat. The leaves can also be dried.

Culture

Sweet marjoram is a tender perennial that grows about one and a half feet tall. In cold climates it is grown as an annual or overwintered indoors. It prefers full sun and well-drained, light-textured, rather dry soil.

It can be propagated from seed in the spring or by division in spring and autumn.

Potato Pie

1 tablespoon oil

2 pounds potatoes (about 6 medium), peeled and diced

1 medium onion, chopped

2 teaspoons chopped marjoram leaves

1 teaspoon chopped parsley leaves

2 eggs

2 cups plain yogurt

Heat the oil in a skillet and sauté the potatoes and onions until golden. Add the herbs, mix thoroughly, and place in a buttered casserole dish, pressing the potatoes level with a spatula. Mix the eggs and yogurt and pour evenly over the potatoes. Bake at 375 degrees for 40 minutes, or until top is browned. Serves 6.

> Love the things nearest at hand; and love intensely. If I were to write a motto over the gate of a garden, I should choose the remark which Socrates made as he saw the luxuries in the market, "How much there is in the world that I do not want!" ✽ LHB

SWEET WOODRUFF   *Rubiaceae family*

Sweet Woodruff
(*Galium odoratum*)

Sweet woodruff is a low-growing perennial with star-shaped leaves. It bears small white flowers in the spring but is more valued for its leaves, which can be dried and used in sachets. The perfume industry uses sweet woodruff to add "forest" tones to fragrances. The leaves also provide the traditional flavoring for May wine.

Sweet woodruff reaches a modest height of six to twelve inches but can be very immodest in its greed for garden space. It spreads readily enough to be called invasive. Partial or fully shaded areas of the garden unsuited for more demanding plants provide the perfect site for this eager herb.

To use the leaves, cut them in spring before the dainty white flowers appear and dry them in a cool place out of direct sun. The leaves have no fragrance when fresh but release the sweet smell of mown hay when dry. They can be sewn into sachets and put in drawers and closets to keep out musty smells.

Dried leaves of sweet woodruff make a stimulating tea.

Culture

A woodland plant in its natural setting, low-growing sweet woodruff likes acid soil. It does not require fertilizing, but it should be cut back after blooming to encourage bushiness. Woodruff can be propagated by division in spring, by stem cuttings, or by seed.

Tansy   *Compositae family*

Tansy
(Tanacetum vulgare)

Tansy was one of the herbs believed to confer immortality, hence its Greek name *athanatos*. Ancients used it in embalming; medievalists used it to protect against the plague and to deworm children.

This pretty herb with its yellow, buttonlike flowers was very popular mixed with eggs and served as a tansy, or Easter custard, in the spring. Today, pungent-flavored tansy has little use in the kitchen. The leaves contain a toxic oil, and many herbalists recommend not using it for flavoring or tea.

It is very decorative, however, and a pretty addition to the garden, with its deeply incised leaves and yellow flowers. The flowers dry well, and the leaves can be put into drawers and closets to help repel insects.

Culture

A perennial that grows to four feet in height, tansy does best in full sun and average garden soil. The stems may require staking, and the roots are moderately invasive; give it plenty of space in the garden. The bright yellow flowers are produced in late July to early September.

Tansy can be propagated from seed or division, and it self-sows.

The variety Crispum has more attractive, fine-cut foliage than the species and is better suited for garden use.

> One never knows a plant until one grows it and cares for it from first to last in all vicissitudes. The satisfaction of seeing a plant spring up, grow, produce its own kind of foliage, take its place among other plants, meet the days and seasons as they pass, is beyond all measure.   ✱ LHB

Thyme (*Thymus*)

THYME *Labiatae family*

I know a bank whereon the wild thyme blows,
Where oxslips and the nodding violet grows,
Quite overcanopied with lush woodbine,
With sweet musk-rose and with englantine.

—Shakespeare, A Midsummer Night's Dream, Act 2, scene 2

There are many different species and cultivars of this fragrant little herb, including shrubs and creepers, lemon- or caraway-flavored thymes, and light-, mid-, and dark-green-leafed varieties. No herb garden is complete without one or several thymes in it, but Narrow Leaf French is one of the preferred cultivars.

Perhaps there are so many varieties because there are so many uses for thyme. *Thymus vulgaris* is an essential ingredient of bouquet garni, the traditional French flavoring for soups, stews, stocks, fish, meat dishes, stuffings, sausages, and cheese. Thyme adds a piquant flavor to butter, jelly, vinegar, and honey.

Thyme is one of the most important culinary herbs, said to be an appetite stimulant, a digestive aid, and especially useful in the digestion of fatty foods such as pork, goose, and sausage.

A tea made with thyme leaves eases digestive problems and may soothe sore throats and coughs because the herb has antiseptic properties. Thyme baths (throw a handful of bruised leaves into the bath water or strain them under the tap through cheesecloth) are said to ease bruises, swellings, sprains, rheumatic problems, and neurasthenia. Thyme has mild stimulating properties, and the leaves can be used fresh or dried.

Thyme attracts bees and is excellent for helping to pollinate the garden. It's also a good companion plant for cabbages, helping to deter worms. Medieval gardeners planted thyme in pathways and on benches, where its fragrance would be released when it was trod upon or touched.

Other Thymes

Lemon Thyme (*Thymus x citriodorus*) is a low, shrubby, evergreen perennial with a lemon scent. Variants include Argenteus, with silver variegated leaves, Aureus, with yellow variegated leaves, and Silver Queen, with silver margins on its leaves.

Lemon thyme
thymus x citriodorus

Bouquet Garni

Fresh or dried herbs can be used. If they are dried, use less because dried herbs tend to have stronger flavor.

4 sprigs parsley (chervil can also be used)

1 bay leaf

2 sprigs thyme

Combine the herbs and tie them into a 4-inch square of cheesecloth. Add during the last 20 minutes of cooking time. Can be used to flavor soups and stews.

THYME *Labiatae family*

Caraway Thyme *(Thymus herba-barona)* is a prostrate thyme that only reaches about five inches in height. Its dark green foliage and showy purple flowers make it a very attractive ground cover. The caraway-flavored leaves are a good flavoring for roast beef.

Mother-of-Thyme *(Thymus praeox ssp. arcticus)* is a very low, prostrate thyme, sometimes also listed as *Thymus serpyllum*. It, too, makes a good ground cover, especially on sunny banks.

Woolly Thyme *(Thymus pseudolanuginosus)* is similar to mother-of-thyme, but its leaves are covered with long white hairs, giving the plant an overall gray color. It is most effective when planted in small pockets of soil between stepping-stones or rock walls and allowed to spread naturally.

Common Thyme *(Thymus vulgaris)* grows to a foot in height and has a pungent, spicy scent. It is the thyme most commonly used in cooking. Its leaves and flowering tops can be added to almost any savory dish or put in sachets, potpourris, and tea. It grows as a compact accent plant for the front of the border or rock garden.

Culture

An evergreen shrub that grows three to fifteen inches tall, thyme likes full sun and sandy, dry soil. In cold climates it should be protected over the winter by mulching with evergreen boughs; the variegated varieties are not as hardy as the nonvariegated ones.

Thymus vulgaris can be started from seed in the early summer, cuttings in mid-spring or early summer, or root divisions in spring. The seeds require temperatures of 70 degrees for germination. Silver- and golden-edged types divide easily if the whole plant is lifted and a cluster of stems, with root attached, is separated. Space the plants nine inches apart.

New plants grow slowly at first and usually do not flower until the second summer. Some varieties, especially lemon or *T. vulgaris*, can be grown indoors as pot plants if they receive strong, direct light. Pinch the tops regularly and prune back older, woody growth each spring.

Thymus praecox sub species arcticus 'Albus'

TRUE LAVENDER *Labiatae family*

True Lavender
Lavandula angustifolia
(L. vera; L. officinalis)

Sleep Pillow

Loosely woven linen, enough to make a pillow about 10 inches square

2 cups dried lavender flowers

1 cup dried lemon balm

1 cup thyme

Stitch the linen into a 10-inch-square pillow, leaving part of one side open. Fill with the herbs and sew closed. Make a separate, washable cover of white or flowered cotton.

Lavender is another popular herb grown today for its fragrance and decorative value rather than for medicinal or culinary purposes. Its fresh, sweet scent has been a favorite perfume throughout history, used in everything from hair rinses to soaps. Its name comes from the Latin *lavare*, to wash.

Place bunches of dried lavender in with clothes and linens to keep them sweet and fresh smelling and to repel insects. In winter, add lavender to dried floral arrangements for color and scent, or simply hang bunches from the ceiling.

Medieval people believed lavender would help protect them from illness and often wore silk bags of lavender around their necks. Victorian women treated headaches by bathing the forehead and wrists with a wash of lavender cologne. Lavender is an excellent addition to potpourris and herb pillows.

An infusion of lavender flowers, made by pouring one cup of boiling water over several stalks of lavender and letting it steep for five minutes, is calming and may also ease a headache. Lavender flowers can be crystallized, like violets, and used as pastry decorations.

Culture

True lavender is a shrubby, semievergreen perennial that grows one to three feet tall. It has small leaves covered with white hairs that give the plant a grayish tinge, and it produces narrow spikes of flowers from late June through July. Although lavender flowers are traditionally a rich, purple-blue color, a white variant (Alba), deep purple variant (Hidcote), and even pink variant (Jean Davis) are also available.

The herb can be grown as a short hedge and maintains some color well into the winter. It's also pretty in the rock garden or perennial border.

Lavender is most easily grown from stem cuttings or division because the seeds germinate slowly and may not breed true to type. The plant likes full sun and light, well-drained, alkaline soil, but it will tolerate dry, poor soil. Prune each year in the spring or after flowering to maintain the shape of the plants.

Because lavender is so soothing, it has long been popular in herbal sleep pillows to help induce a good night's rest.

The proper caretaking of the earth lies not alone in maintaining its fertility or in safeguarding its products. The lines of beauty that appeal to the eye and the charm that satisfies the five senses are in our keeping.

WILD MARJORAM   *Labiatae family*

Wild Marjoram/ Oregano (*Origanum vulgare*)

The herb we commonly call oregano is really one of several species of wild marjoram, the most commonly used one being Greek oregano (O. *vulgare*, subspecies *hirtum*).

Oregano is one of the mainstays of the kitchen, and with good reason. Its distinct flavoring enhances tomato dishes, meat, poultry and pork stuffing, vegetables, and egg dishes. To give grilled meats and fish a pleasant flavor, lay stems of oregano over the coals.

Tea made from the leaves or the flowering tops can ease indigestion, headaches, and nervousness.

Culture

Wild marjoram, or oregano, is an erect perennial that grows two and a half feet tall and produces purple spikelets of flowers from July through September.

In full sun with well-drained soil the plant will self-sow prolifically, or it can be propagated by seed, stem cuttings, or division. Divide the plants every two or three years.

Different variants avaliable include Aureum, with yellow leaves and white flowers, and Viride, with green bracts and white flowers.

A border or free mass of perennial herbs is one of the charms of any place. It is informal, easy of care, and self-sustaining. ✸ LHB

WINTER SAVORY *Labiatae family*

Winter Savory
(*Satureja montana*)

This peppery perennial has a sharper flavor than summer savory, but it is easier to grow than its annual cousin. Native to the Mediterranean region, it will thrive in poor, coarse soil and does not need much water. In fact, too much water will decrease its winter hardiness.

Like summer savory, winter savory was believed to be a stimulant and aphrodisiac. The leaves can be used to flavor meat, fish, poultry, salad, soup, stew, and sausages. The flowering tops can be made into a tea that aids digestion and stimulates the appetite. Or it can be used to make an antiseptic gargle to ease a sore throat.

Semievergreen, the herb is attractive grown in the rock garden or front of the perennial border. In early July it produces small, white flowers that contrast nicely with the dark green foliage.

Culture

Winter savory is a perennial that grows about one foot tall. It has a slightly spreading growth habit and needlelike, dark green foliage.

It can be grown from seed or propagated by stem cuttings, layering, or division. It likes full sun and light, rather dry, well-drained soil. It may rot in poorly drained sites.

The plants lose their vitality as they age so start a new crop of winter savory every other year. Prune the plants in spring but avoid overharvesting close to winter.

Of gardens there are many kinds. The forms are as many as the gardeners. No activity is more adaptable to one's essential wishes and moods. ✻ LHB

YARROW/MILFOIL   *Compositae family*

Yarrow/Milfoil
(Achillea millefolium)

This hardy, useful, and lovely herb was first brought to America by the English colonists, who planted it in their gardens. From those gardens it has spread as a wildflower to meadows and roadsides.

Its name, *Achillea*, attests to its legendary fame as a healing plant. Achilles was believed to use the herb to heal his warriors after the battle of Troy. Applied on a wound, it is said to stanch the flow of blood. In China, stalks of yarrow were used in conjunction with the *I Ching* for telling the future.

Gardeners today find the plant very useful. Bits of leaves thrown in the compost will help decomposition. If planted near ailing plants, the root secretions of yarrow may help heal them.

But many gardeners grow yarrow simply for its beauty. In addition to the common white yarrow, it is also available in many pretty pastel colors, ranging from yellow to rose. The flowers dry very well and make long-lasting winter bouquets.

Try a tea made from dried leaves for indigestion (they have a mild flavor similar to sage) or an infusion of flowers for a face lotion.

Culture

Yarrow is a hardy perennial that does well in sunny or lightly shaded spots. It likes moderately rich, moist soil and may become invasive.

Sow from seed or divide roots in spring or autumn. The flowers last a long time in the garden, and deadheading the blooms as they fade may yield a second flowering.

Some varieties of yarrow grow up to a sprawling four feet in height; others stay more compact at about two feet.

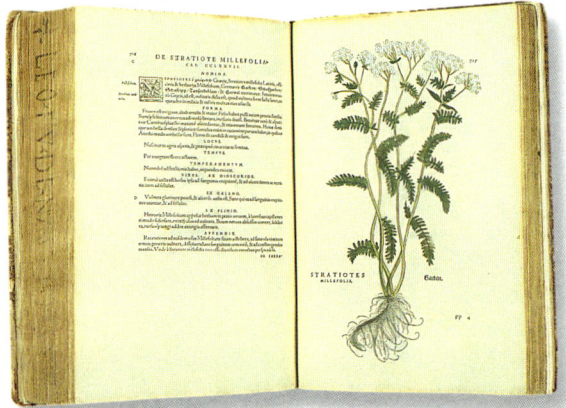

Yarrow as depicted by Leonhart Fuchs, in his 1542 herbal De Historia Stirpium, *from the Rare and Manuscript Collection, Cornell University Library.*

Yarrows are grown in borders and the smaller species in rock-gardens, and bloom in spring and summer, often lasting until autumn. They are of easy culture. ✽ LHB

The following herbs, described in the previous section, also have edible flowers:

Anise Hyssop—*Agastache foeniculum*
Borage—*Borago officinalis*
Chives—*Allium schoenoprasum*
Clary Sage—*Salvia sclarea*
Common Fennel—*Foeniculum vulgare*
Garden Sage—*Salvia officinalis*
Hyssop—*Hyssopus officinalis*
Mint—*Mentha*
Rosemary—*Rosmarinus officinalis*
Scented Geranium—*Pelargonium*
Sweet Basil—*Ocimum basilicum*
Wild Marjoram/Oregano—*Origanum vulgare*

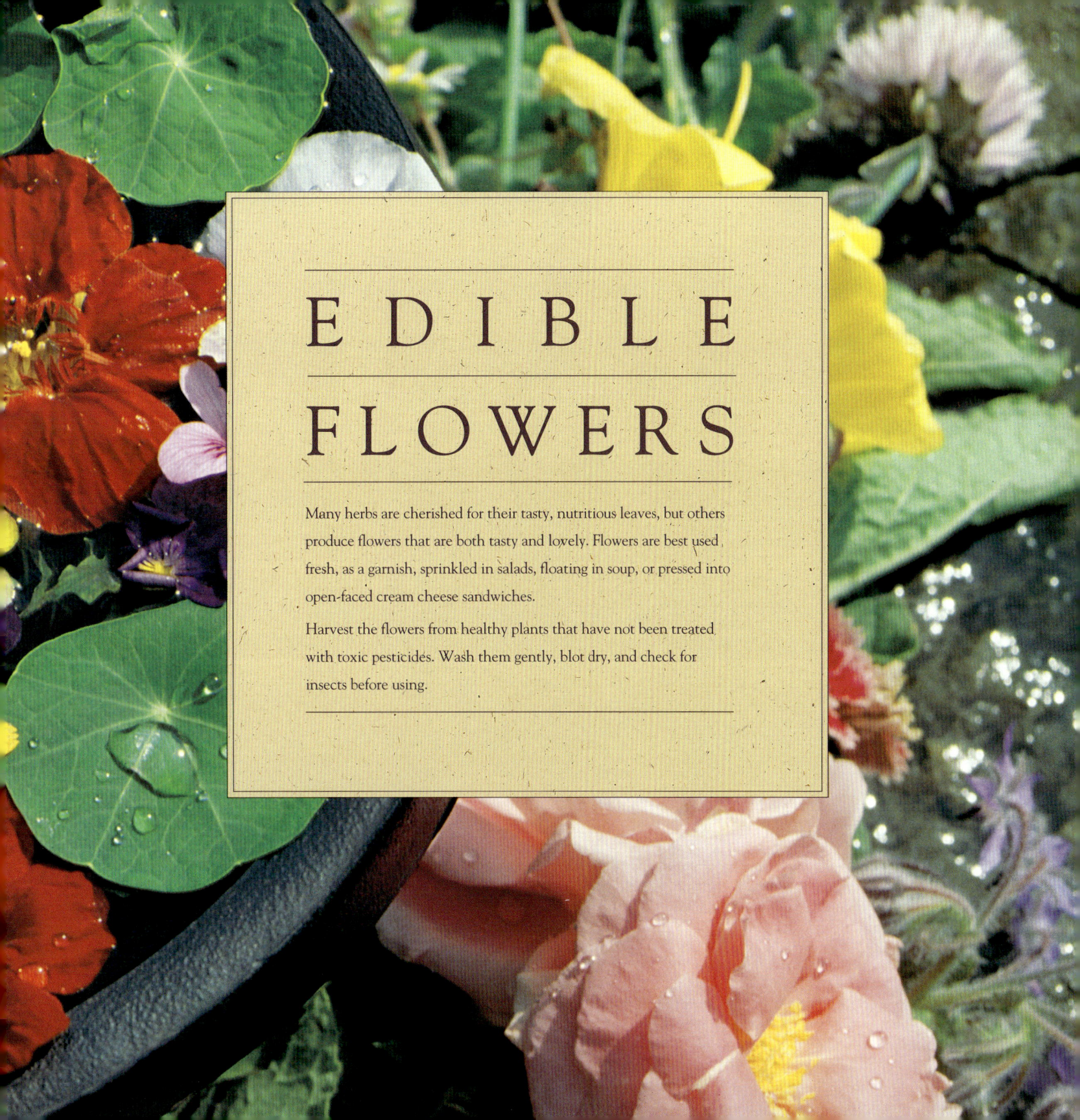

EDIBLE FLOWERS

Many herbs are cherished for their tasty, nutritious leaves, but others produce flowers that are both tasty and lovely. Flowers are best used fresh, as a garnish, sprinkled in salads, floating in soup, or pressed into open-faced cream cheese sandwiches.

Harvest the flowers from healthy plants that have not been treated with toxic pesticides. Wash them gently, blot dry, and check for insects before using.

BEE BALM   *Labiatae family*

Bee Balm
(*Monarda didyma*)

Native to North America, this perennial is also sometimes known as Oswego tea. The leaves have a mild mint flavor. Colonists learned of its use as a tea herb from Indians. It became one of the herbs popular as a substitute for China tea after the Boston Tea Party.

In summer, the plant produces shaggy red, lavender, white, or pink flowers that can be added to salads or used as a garnish.

Monarda is a perennial that will grow in sun or part shade, reaching two or three feet in height. Start with named varieties, and then propagate by division.

CALENDULA/POT MARIGOLD *Compositae family*

Calendula/Pot Marigold
(*Calendula officinalis*)

Just looking upon these sunny, yellow flowers was said to draw evil humors out of the head and strengthen the eyesight. Marigold was said to protect against poisoning, intestinal trouble, scabs, plague, and bad temper.

Add marigold petals to soups and stews, or use raw in salads.

Calendula is an annual that grows one to two feet tall. Plant in full sun. Seedlings can be started indoors and then transplanted into the garden in spring.

DAYLILY   *Liliaceae family*

Daylily
(*Hemerocallis*)

These perennials are easy to grow and provide beautiful summer blooms in shades of yellow, orange, red, or pink. Each flower lasts a single day, but the tall stems bear several buds so that the plants bloom over a good length of time.

Pick individual flowers to use in salads or garnishings, or try stuffing the blooms with soft cheese for an appetizer.

Different daylilies grow from eighteen inches to several feet tall and bloom at various times of the garden cycle. Plant in sun or part shade, dividing the clumps every three or four years.

Nasturtium   *Tropaeolaceae family*

Nasturtium
(*Tropaeolum majus*)

Nasturtium, brought back to England from the New World, has been grown ever since as a salad green in English gardens. It has round leaves and brightly colored spurred flowers with a mild, peppery flavor. Its name is from the Latin for "twisted nose," referring to its peppery flavor.

An annual, nasturtium grows easily from seed sown in place in the garden. Plant three-quarters of an inch deep when soil is warm; avoid transplanting. It likes sun and poor soil. Do not fertilize nasturtium!

Dwarf nasturtium grows about ten inches tall. Climbers may grow to six feet and are especially attractive for boxes and hanging baskets.

No flower makes a finer display in vase or bowl than these rich colors, all harmonizing well and lighting up a room as very few of the common easily grown flowers do. ✸ LHB

Rose   *Rosaceae family*

Rose
(*Rosa*)

Although we most enjoy roses for their beauty and scent, they have also played an important role in many different cuisines. Medieval cooks mixed roses with saffron, almonds, and capon to make a rosee; Victorian hostesses served rose-flavored sugar with tea; and some Middle Eastern dishes, especially sweets, are still flavored with rose.

Any roses served, rather than merely displayed, should be organically grown. This rules out florists' flowers.

To serve roses in salad, wash the flowers and gently tear the petals off the stem, mixing them with the greens. If the slightly bitter flavor seems unpleasant, cut away the white base at each petal.

To flavor sugar, layer rose petals in the sugar jar.

Roses are herbaceous shrubs that are less than carefree to grow but well worth the trouble. Begin with a good garden catalog and pick out a few of the old-fashioned varieties for your herb garden such as R. Damascena and R. Gallica, then carefully follow planting and maintenance directions.

A selection of roses offered in the Spring 1892 catalog of Green's Nursery Company, Rochester, New York.

It seems to be the first desire of the home maker, when he considers the planting of his grounds, to set out Roses. ✽ LHB

Viola   Violaceae family

Viola: Sweet Violet
(Viola odorata)

Johnny Jump-Up
(Viola tricolor)

Pansy
(Viola x Wittrockiana)

Medievalists used violets in salads, sauces, omelets, fritters, custards, and cakes. Today, candied violets are a welcome decoration on pastries and confections. Add a handful of purple or white violets to salads, garnish grilled meats with fresh pansies, or top a cake with pretty violas.

In the garden, all three violas will tolerate some shade. Sweet violet is a perennial that multiplies quickly. Pansies and violas are also perennial, but they are tender and usually grown as annuals. They can be started from seed in the garden, or seedlings can be started indoors and transplanted into the garden.

Pick the flowers regularly and don't let them go to seed to encourage blooms. Fertilize several times during the growing season.

Pansies delight in cool weather and moisture.

N O T E S

> I staid home from a vacation one summer that I might keep my plants from dying. I have since learned that if the plants in my borders cannot take care of themselves for a few weeks, they are little comfort to me.
> ✻ LHB

NOTES

One must first seek to love plants and nature, and then to cultivate that happy peace of mind which is satisfied with little. He will be happier if he has no rigid and arbitrary ideals, for gardens are coquettish, particularly with the novice. ✸ LHB

N O T E S

> The [parsley] seed is slow to germinate, and often the second or third sowing is made, thinking the first is a failure; but usually after what would seem a long time the young plants will be seen.
> ✸ LHB

N O T E S

> We express vast pride in the achievements of our labor, but it is the good employment of leisure that makes persons and peoples great . . . the real utilization of leisure is to have resources where one lives; gardening is one of these real resources. ✲ LHB